Translocal Performance in Asian Theatre and Film

Iris H. Tuan

Translocal Performance in Asian Theatre and Film

palgrave
macmillan

Iris H. Tuan
National Chiao Tung University
Jhubei City, Hsinchu, Taiwan

ISBN 978-981-10-8608-3   ISBN 978-981-10-8609-0 (eBook)
https://doi.org/10.1007/978-981-10-8609-0

Library of Congress Control Number: 2018942632

© The Editor(s) (if applicable) and The Author(s) 2018
This work is subject to copyright. All rights are solely and exclusively licensed by the Publisher, whether the whole or part of the material is concerned, specifically the rights of translation, reprinting, reuse of illustrations, recitation, broadcasting, reproduction on microfilms or in any other physical way, and transmission or information storage and retrieval, electronic adaptation, computer software, or by similar or dissimilar methodology now known or hereafter developed.
The use of general descriptive names, registered names, trademarks, service marks, etc. in this publication does not imply, even in the absence of a specific statement, that such names are exempt from the relevant protective laws and regulations and therefore free for general use.
The publisher, the authors, and the editors are safe to assume that the advice and information in this book are believed to be true and accurate at the date of publication. Neither the publisher nor the authors or the editors give a warranty, express or implied, with respect to the material contained herein or for any errors or omissions that may have been made. The publisher remains neutral with regard to jurisdictional claims in published maps and institutional affiliations.

Cover credit: Détail de la Tour Eiffel © nemesis2207/Fotolia.co.uk

Printed on acid-free paper

This Palgrave Pivot imprint is published by the registered company Springer Nature Singapore Pte Ltd. part of Springer Nature.
The registered company address is: 152 Beach Road, #21-01/04 Gateway East, Singapore 189721, Singapore

*This book is dedicated to my parents
Father Tuan Shi-Ge (1924–2004)
Mother Yang Shu-Yu (1938–2002)*

ACKNOWLEDGMENTS

I feel grateful for many people's help, support, and encouragement during the difficulties and hardships in my life. This book is brand new, collecting seven years of research after numerous revisions based on my accumulated material from my summer of research in 2011 at Berkeley University, as Visiting Scholar (chosen to be sent by Top University Strategic Alliance of Taiwan) for one year in the Department of English at Harvard University and Fairbank Center from 2012 to 2013, and what I have recently written, as well as my teaching and academic services at National Chiao Tung University from 2013 to 2018.

Almost all of the chapters in this book have been presented in their preliminary draft states at international conferences, including American Society for Theatre Research (ASTR), Association for Theatre in Higher Education (ATHE), Association for Asian Performance (AAP), among others, but until now have not been formally published. The expert and valuable comments from professors and professionals have provided me with very useful feedback, which has helped me to revise, polish, cut, and embellish to create this book. Only a few of the book chapters have had very small portions of the short performance reviews published in some influential flagship international journals. I appreciate Asian Theatre Journal (ATJ) Editor Kathy Foley's excellent editing of my performance reviews for *My Daughter's Wedding*, CLT's *A Midsummer Night's Dream*, and the Hakka musical *Xiangsi Nostalgia*, published in *Asian Theatre Journal* (A & HCI). I have fair use to integrate my three short reviews into my full-length chapters.

It is great that this manuscript can finally be published to share with you, my dear readers, friends, and relatives my research expertise and interesting knowledge from Western theory, Asian performance, and film. I hope you enjoy the fruitful insights and wisdom in this book and that it will inspire you in your life.

Special thanks go to Sara Crowley-Vigneau, Editor, Connie Li, Editorial Assistant at Palgrave Macmillan, ArunPrakash Ramasamy and the Production Team in Springer Nature. Thanks to my part-time assistant Anna Chang, who helped with the page formatting from April to May 2017. Thanks also to Edison Lee, my part-time assistant, who helped me to get the figure permission from those relevant directors and troupes from December 2017 to January 2018.

Last but not least, the incessant unspoken support from my family and beloved is highly appreciated. Without you, I cannot make it.

Translocal Performance in Asian Theatre and Film will be of interest to students and scholars of theater and performance studies, film and media studies, visual culture, cultural creative industry, Asian studies, cultural studies, and musical theater.

Contents

1 Introduction   1

2 Methodologies: From Postcolonial Feminism and Creolization Toward Translocal   11

Part I   Intercultural Theatre in Taiwan   19

3 Contemporary Legend Theatre's *A Midsummer Night's Dream*: Tradition, Modernity, and Translocality   21

4 Yukio Ninagawa's *Hamlet* in Taiwan: Intercultural Representation   37

5 Theater Represents Literature: Love and Labor in *To Send Away Under Escort*   51

Part II   From Local to Global: Hakka, Dance, Chinese Musical, and Film   61

6 Change of Hakka Opera: Ethnicity and Creation in Hakka Musical and Hakka TV Drama   63

7	Hakka Culture and Image in Film and Performance	97
8	Irresistible Seduction and Translocal Labor of Musical Theater in Taiwan: From Translation to Multi-arts	105
9	Spectacle, Adaptation, and Sexuality in Chinese Musicals	125
10	The Abject, Murder, and Sex in *The Great Buddha+*	139
11	Sex, Money, Calculation, and Manipulation in Politics in *The Bold, The Corrupt, and The Beautiful*	151
12	Conclusion	161
Bibliography		165
Index		175

List of Figures

Fig. 3.1   Cast and the team group photo. CLT's *A Midsummer Night's Dream* (March 2016, National Theater in Taipei). (Courtesy of CLT)   26

Fig. 3.2   Fairy King (played by Wu Hsing-Kuo in golden yellow costume) and Fairy Queen (played by Wei Hai-Min in silver white costume) have a quarrel over the ownership of the cute boy in the forest scene. CLT's *A Midsummer Night's Dream* (March 2016, National Theater in Taipei). (Courtesy of CLT)   31

Fig. 4.1   The the Mouse Trap scene is staged for the second time in this play-within-the-play-within-the-play in Ninagawa's *Hamlet* (2015) in spectacular beautiful royal court costumes and elegant movement in Japanese *kabuki* style. (Courtesy of Takahiro Watanabe)   40

Fig. 4.2   Wearing a black long robe, Tatsuya Fujiwara's interpretation of Hamlet, with the hint of Oedipus Complex, is more violent than Sir Laurence Olivier's portrayal of a more classic and melancholy Hamlet (1948 film). (Courtesy of Takahiro Watanabe)   42

Fig. 5.1   Actor Tang Tsung-Sheng (playing the role of Pickpocket Ho) performs the magic tricks of escaping from the handcuffs and the rope on stage (left). The naïve Hwang (the role is played by Huang Di-Yang) (right). (Courtesy of Greenray Theatre Company)   53

Fig. 5.2   Actor Tang (playing the role of pickpocket Ho), kneeling down to express his filial piety, finally meets his adopted grandmother who is old, sick, and near dying. In the center right, Ray Fan plays the role of the old Grandma. To the left, the good, naïve

xi

rookie policeman (played by Huang Di-Yang) is moved to agree to accompany Ho to pay the visit and then escort him back to the prison. On the right, Orange (played by actress Dai Hsui-Yin), who is in love with Ho, waits for him, taking care of his grandma for many years. (Courtesy of Greenray Theatre Company) 56

Fig. 6.1 *My Daughter's Wedding* used traditional Hakka dress. (Courtesy of Hakka Affairs Council of Taiwan) 73

Fig. 6.2 *My Daughter's Wedding*'s production numbers featured modern elements like dancers in T-shirts and with motorcycles. (Courtesy of Hakka Affairs Council of Taiwan) 76

Fig. 6.3 *The Yang's Ninth Sister*, Hakka TV drama, is performed by Sin-Yong-Guang Troupe. (Courtesy of Hakka Affairs Council of Taiwan) 87

Fig. 7.1 Film poster of *My Native Land*. Retrieved from www.city.fukuoka.lg.jp (Courtesy of Lee Hsing) 99

Fig. 7.2 The dancers dance while the singers sing a duet on the roof to celebrate Hakka community lives. (Courtesy of Neo-Classic Dance Company) 101

Fig. 7.3 The dancers dance well and the singers sing touching Hakka songs. Together they weave a good and simple picture of that earlier Hakka agricultural time in the live stage performance. (Courtesy of Neo-Classic Dance Company) 102

Fig. 8.1 *Kiss Me Nana*. New Millennium Version (1999–2000). (Courtesy of Godot Theatre) 108

Fig. 8.2 The Taiwanese aborigine young man sings of his despair and hope in the musical *See the Sun*. (Courtesy of Godot Theatre) 110

Fig. 8.3 Composer Deng Yu-Hsien and the singer's love story in *April Rain*. (Courtesy of All Music Theater) 112

Fig. 8.4 The musical *Mulan* was inspired by and adapted from the animated film. (Courtesy of Director Lu Poshen, Tainan Jen Theatre, and Photographer Chen, Yu-Wei) 113

Fig. 8.5 Jolin Tsai and Pao-Chang Tsai's *PK* (2015). (Courtesy of National Theatre) 116

Fig. 8.6 The cast in the Hakka musical "*Xiangsi Nostalgia*" (《香絲相思》) (2016, Taipei). (Courtesy of Hakka Affairs Council) 117

Fig. 8.7 The lovers in the Hakka musical "*Xiangsi Nostalgia*" (《香絲相思》) (2016, Taipei). (Courtesy of Hakka Affairs Council) 117

Fig. 8.8 Pingmei (平妹 Flat Girl)'s wedding in the Hakka Musical *Xiangsi Nostalgia* (2016, Taipei). (Courtesy of Hakka Affairs Council) 120

Fig. 9.1 The wars between Yan Emperor's general tribe chief Chi-Yo and his soldiers and the Yellow Emperor's troupe. (Courtesy of NTNU) 134

LIST OF FIGURES   xiii

Fig. 9.2   Nu Wa (女媧, Goddess Mother Earth in Chinese mythology) ascended into the air, with the aid of the suspension machine system, and the rotating stage turned, then the crowds of people went on stage. (Courtesy of NTNU) 135
Fig. 10.1   The murder scene. (Courtesy of Photographer Liu, Chen-hsiang) 140
Fig. 10.2   The two nobodies Belly Bottom (played by Chen Chu-Sheng) (right) and Prickle (played by Chuang Yi-Zeng) (left) in *The Great Buddha+* watch Pricke's rich boss having sex in his car on the dashcam videos. (Courtesy of Creamfilm Production) 141
Fig. 10.3   Poor Belly Bottom lives in poverty. (Courtesy of Photographer Liu, Chen-hsiang) 142
Fig. 10.4   The rich businessmen and powerful politicians' sex and wine party in the big Jacuzzi in their private club. (Courtesy of Creamfilm Production) 143
Fig. 10.5   The monks' and the crowd's lengthy chanting in the ritual is stopped by the gradually louder and louder strange sound coming from the inside of the Big Buddha where Madame Yeh knocks to cry out for justice. (Courtesy of Photographer Liu, Chen-hsiang) 144
Fig. 10.6   The voice of the dead Belly Bottom. (Courtesy of Creamfilm Production) 147
Fig. 10.7   Ironically, the powerful politician can threaten the policeman into dropping his investigation of the rich businessman. (Courtesy of Creamfilm Production) 148
Fig. 11.1   The poster of the film *The Bold, The Corrupt, and The Beautiful*. The three leading actresses are from Hong Kong and Taiwan. The youngest actress is studying and pursuing her career in China now. (Courtesy of Yang Ya-Jie) 153
Fig. 11.2   The young fourteen-year-old Tang Chen watches from the window while Tang Ning is having sex with the two gangsters. (Courtesy of Yang Ya-Jie) 154
Fig. 11.3   The fantasy love triangle scene in the forest. (Courtesy of Yang Ya-Jie) 156
Fig. 11.4   The blind storytelling narrators (including Taiwan Treasure Yang Hsiu-ching) in the TV studio's frame within the film frame tell and comment on Tang's family story. (Courtesy of Yang Ya-Jie) 158
Fig. 11.5   The hospital scene. (Courtesy of Yang Ya-Jie) 159

CHAPTER 1

Introduction

Abstract This book, in the theoretical translocality, illuminates contemporary intercultural theater, Asian performance—Hakka, dance, Chinese musical, and Asian film (including the two 2017 Golden Horse Awards winners). More than fourteen case studies are explored, including CLT's *A Midsummer Night's Dream* (2016), Yukio Ninagawa's *Hamlet* (2015), *To Send Away Under Escort* (2015), Hakka musical *My Daughter's Wedding* (2007), Hakka TV drama *The Ninth Sister of Yang* (2009), the film *My Native Land* (1980), Neo-Classic Dance Company's "The Drifting Fate of Hakka" (2014), the music concert (2015), the Chinese musical *Mulan* (2011), Jolin and Pao's *PK* (2015), Hakka musical *Xiangsi Nostalgia* (2016), the musical *Mountains and Seas* (restaged 2017), the black-and-white film *The Great Buddha+* (2017), and the film *The Bold, The Corrupt, and The Beautiful* (2017).

Keywords Translocal • Performance • Asian • Theater • Dance • Film

In the perspective of translocal performance, this book covers contemporary intercultural theater, Peking opera innovation, Japanese performance, Taiwan literature theater, Chinese performance, Hakka opera, Hakka TV drama, Hakka film, Hakka dance, Hakka musical, Chinese musical theater, and Asian films, (including the two 2017 Golden Horse Awards winners), staged and produced in Taiwan. In an innovative way, it explores the minority's ethnicity story, such as through Hakka opera, Hakka musical,

Hakka TV drama, and Hakka film, which were previously unknown or neglected. In the Asian theater scholar's perspective, based on the Republic of Formosa, the beautiful treasure island in the Pacific Ocean, I examine the theater performing arts and film in terms of aesthetics, gender studies, and identity politics while facing the tremendous changes in the e-era driven by advanced technology, such as the introduction of robots and artificial intelligence. By writing about recent representative artistic works, this book endeavors to retain the irresistible value of human accomplishments in theater and film.

THEATRICALIZING TRANSLATION: LITERATURE, PERFORMANCE, AND FILM

In the twenty-first century, as the boundaries within and between nation-states shift, we may link the transnational and the translocal so that the dimensions of human beings' experiences can be more sufficiently conveyed. The rapid socioeconomic changes in this century—including the pervasiveness of digital technologies, migrations, climate change, the economic recession, the potential shift in world economic power from Europe and the US toward, quite possibly, China, a range of post-9/11 issues, ISIS, anti-terrorism, North Korea's nuclear bomb, extreme climate, and so on—are transforming and unsettling our understanding of geopolitical time and space, and of the use of the theatrical and the literary in glocalization empowered by swift information exchange through social media and global news. Therefore, we need new perspectives that chart these emerging mobile geographies and new methodologies of interpreting the performance in Asian theater and film.

This book *Translocal Performance in Asian Theater and Film* has the trajectory from postcolonial history to the postmodern information e-era. In the theoretical perspective of translocality, I explore the nuances and complexity of several Asian performances and three Asian films. Aside from the Introduction and Conclusion, there are ten main chapters in this book.

CHAPTER 2

Arjun Appadurai's concept of diaspora and "scapes" contributes to the creation of translocal theory. Similarly, in the critical anthology *Land/Scape/Theater* co-edited with Elinor Fuchs, Una Chaudhuri's notion of geopathology "in translocal social action" (2002, p. 8) also links scape and land in relation to theater.

While we must not deflate the importance of the translocal phenomenon, it should remind us how we are embedded in the world and the discourses within which we examine the translocal performance histories. Responses are embedded in translocal movements across places, time, and people as constructing dynamic cultural flows. In this book, translocality is utilized in the production of cultural practices, particularly contemporary Taiwanese, Chinese, and Japanese intercultural theater, Chinese musical theater, and Asian film.

In terms of the translocal, Chinese modernities can be explored in Asian diaspora and transnational relocation. In diaspora, Chinese modernity can be achieved through translocal experiences. In transnational capitalism, Asian theater, was originally imagined as the Other. Some stereotypes might be mobilized through media, as in musical theater and film. Exoticism, ideology, and cosmopolitanism play on the visual images while we conceptualize the nature of Asian identity and modernity in those major cities in the world manifested in the translocal performance and film.

New perspectives of the "translocal" help broaden our theoretical and spatial understanding of Asian performances and films to elaborate our expressions of interpreting the significations. To apply the theories to each individual performance and film that is simultaneously and already embodied, intercultural, and translocal.

CHAPTER 3

It is argued that the live performance of Shakespeare's *A Midsummer Night's Dream* in Taipei in 2016, by the Contemporary Legend Theatre (CLT), displays the Asian dream and local cultural imagination, in an eclectic reception. This CLT version of the play, starring actor Wu Hsing-kuo and actress Wei Hai-Min, was intended to interpret the Bard in terms of Asian intercultural Shakespearean performance. The tradition upheld in Chinese Peking opera has often undergone modern innovations.

Shakespeare's plays have been extensively adapted in Asian theater. As Arjun Appadurai in *Modernity at Large: Cultural Dimensions of Globalization* points out, media and migration, as the two elements embodying modern subjectivity, explore the work of imagination. In Appadurai's view the mobile images and the de-territorialized spectators come to confront each other. These images create the public sphere of the diaspora. In diasporic hybridity, one feels, tradition and modernity blend the synchronic and diachronic relationships between human beings and places.

The trans-boundary images in the local Taiwan performance complement the global Shakespearean idiom. The binary opposition between the specific and the universal gradually disappear in the contemporary translocal parlance. It is argued that the live performance of CLT's *A Midsummer Night's Dream*, after the script adaptation and theater representation in cross-country and cross-racial terms, displays the Asian dream and local cultural imagination. A global, cultural mobility appeals to an imaginative community in both a virtual and a real theater space. All of the images, media dynamics and information, manifest a synthesis of Shakespeare's influence and the Chinese Peking opera's heritage in a modern performance statement.

Chapter 4

Across the local boundary, some Japanese directors have been invited to stage their works in Taiwan—the translocal performance imbued with the intercultural meanings. Representing Japan's indelible scenes in the Meiji period, director Yukio Ninagawa (1935–2016) staged *Hamlet* in the National Theater of Taiwan (premiere, March 26, 2015, Taipei). It was performed in Japanese with Chinese subtitles. Faithfully presenting every line of the original play by Shakespeare, Ninagawa's adaptation opens with a stage set designed by Setsu Asakura to project the former's idea of the setting being the Meiji period. This pays tribute to the era when *Hamlet* was first acted on stage in Japan. I explore this Japanese performance along with other Asian and Western intertextual antecedents of production.

In the three layers of the play-within-the-play-within-the-play, Ninagawa represents "the Mouse Trap" scene through a double murder—one in mime (without arousing Claudius' attention as he flirts with Gertrude) and the other by *Shingeki*, the spoken drama in the spectacular Meiji Royal court costumes, blending with the elegant, mise-en-scène movement in Kabuki style—while the Japanese, sadist, torture style colors Claudius's confession scene. The actress playing Ophelia's character sings Japanese songs in a contemporary, Japanese manner, which conveys her fatal discord of the mind. I argue that while Ninagawa uses the actor to ask "Who are you?" in a contemporary idiom in his *Hamlet*, the Western influence, filtered through the concluding duel between Laertes and Hamlet before a Japanese target culture, represents the renewed order of Fortinbras on the threshold of the kingdom as it is in the post-war Japan. I explore this Japanese flavor and argue both authentic Japanese cultural roots and Western—Asian intercultural impact in this production.

Chapter 5

In the local Taiwan, the history is transmitted through time and space to bring nostalgia in the 1950s with the representation of literature in theater. Greenray Theatre Company in Taiwan has, since 1993, staged four kinds of productions: (1) the original musical series, (2) the citizen drama, (3) the world theater, and (4) Taiwan literature theater series. Adapting from Taiwanese literature, this chapter explores love and labor in the stage performance of *To Send Away Under Escort* (押解) (October 31, 2015, Jhubei City Performance Hall). Playwright Wu, Nien-Chen collaborates with Director Li, Ming-Tse, good at comedy, to adapt the novel of the same title written by Mr. Tuan, Tsai-Hua (1933–2015). The story is about a young rookie policeman (played by Huang, Di-Yang) who escorts the tricky pickpocket Ho (played by Tang, Tsung-Sheng)—who's priorities are on family, friendship, and love —from the prison in Kaohsiung to the court in Taipei in order to prevent him from escaping.

Intertextuality is contained by using Peking opera's "Sue-San Being Sent Under Escort" in this stage performance. In a satirical tone, the character Policeman Huang, in his action of sending Ho away under escort, suggests that the protagonist should love and take care of his "fruit garden," an extended metaphor for Ho's harem of mistresses with delicious nicknames like Orange, Litchi, and Peach. The two male lead characters play important, visible roles. However, in a feminist vein, I argue that the not so visible female roles of Orange, Litchi, and Peach and the women, though not protagonists, like the protagonist's grandma, actually propel the plot forward.

The themes of this play are compassion, empathy, law, and love. Except for the two male leads, almost every actor and actress play multiple roles. The set is mainly on a train. Nostalgia and local politics (pre-martial law) are the tools used to appeal to the universal love. Literature can be transformed from different genres, from novel to script, and then into performance, by using the process of adaptation and mixed languages (Mandarin and Taiwanese dialect) as cultural capital in revitalizing Asian performance.

Chapter 6

In translocality, from England in the seventeenth century to Asia in the twenty-first century, what kind of intercultural theater is produced when Shakespeare's England is examined through the prism of Hakka culture? And what local TV Hakka drama program can be created by absorbing the tradition? This chapter explores the live Hakka musical *My Daughter's Wedding* (2007) in the theater, and Hakka drama *The Ninth Sister of Yang* (2009) on TV. The former, the first Hakka musical, is a Shakespearean adaptation of *The Taming of the Shrew*. The latter, an original Hakka drama, performed by Sin-Yong-Guang Troupe, is played on Hakka TV station in Taipei. The way in which Hakka opera has developed into Hakka musical and Hakka drama on TV is a reflection of the translocal culture promulgated by government's local cultural policy and media. In this chapter, I focus on the issue of marriage anxiety through the characters of Liu, Li-Chun (Katherina in Shakespeare's play, played by Actress Hsu, Yan-Ling) and Chung, Yo-Chia (Petruchio in Shakespeare's play, played by Actor Huang, Shi-Wei) in *My Daughter's Wedding* and in *The Ninth Sister of Yang* adaptation to argue how Hakka opera is shifting from traditional to new processes of creation.

Chapter 7

Local ethnicity and minority can be demonstrated in a translocal sense. In this chapter, the portrayal of Hakka culture and images on screen and on stage is explored with the three case studies: the movie *China My Native Land*, adapted from Chung Lihe's short novel (1915–1960); Neo-Classic Dance Company's *The Drifting Fate of Hakka* (2014); and the music concert *Belongingness in Heart is Your Native Land* (2015) held in memory of Chung Lihe. These case studies present aesthetics of simplicity, cultural mobility, love, and belongingness.

The famous and attractive leading actor and actress in *China My Native Land* are used to present the Hakka aesthetics of simplicity, cultural mobility, love, and a sense of belongingness. In the film we see Hakka culture and image represented by cinematography. Chung Lihe, the Hakka writer, was born in Pingtung. Chung fell in love with Chung, Tai-Mei. However, due to the custom that prohibited marriage between two people with the same last name at that time, they eloped via Japan to Shenyang in the north east of China; then came back to Taiwan. In the original short novel *China My Native Land*, Chung describes his longing for and nostalgia toward the ideal native land.

Neo-Classic Dance Company's *The Drifting Fate of Hakka* (December 5–7, 2014, Taipei National Theater), choreographed by Lu, Yi-Chuan, uses dance to portray Hakka immigrants' ethnicity history. Visually it shows the "reverse-the-wind spirit of Hakka ethnicity in the process of constant immigration."[1] This Hakka dance performance also includes storytelling and singing for added theatricality.

The music concert *Belongingness in Heart is Your Native Land*, held on October 24, 2015 at the Hakka Music Theater Center in Taipei, retells Chung's story. Based on Chung's novel, Composer Chou created the concert's music scores for a collaborative performance with the three dancers of Legend Lin Dance Theatre.

The aforementioned three case studies display Hakka culture and images in cinema and theater performing arts (dance and concert), through simple aesthetics of minimalism. I argue that Hakka culture and images are used theatricality in cinema and performances to demonstrate Hakka ethnicity, immigration, belongingness, and cultural mobility.

CHAPTER 8

Applying the theory of translocality and multi-art forms, from global to local, examining performance as labor and labor as performance, musical theater in Taiwan has been importing Broadway musicals for different modes of performing to stage various aesthetic styles. Most rely on translation—usually English into Chinese—for example, *Kiss Me Nana*, produced by the Godot Theatre Company, was translated from the English *Kiss Me Kate*. Few are faithful presentations in English. Some of them are opera and film adaptations; for instance, *Love Ends in Night Shanghai* (2002) adapted from Alexandre Dumas, fils' novel *La Dame aux Camelias*, *Running Angel* (2005) adapted from the film *Sister Act* (1992), *My Daughter's Wedding* (2007) adapted from Shakespeare's *The Taming of the Shrew*, and so on. Some of them are original and innovative local Asian creations; for example, *Snow Wolf Lake* (1997) by the well-known popular Hong Kong singer Jacky H. Cheung (張學友), *See The Sun* (2000) on the Taiwanese aboriginal ethnicity issue, and *April Rain* (2007), the Taiwanese musical on the Hakka composer Deng Yu-Hsien's love story under Japanese colonialization. No matter what form or style it takes, translation is a significant part of staging musical theater in Taiwan. This chapter explores the dynamics between musicals and the interpretations in Asian theater as well as the work involved in translation and the recent trends in musical theater performances in the local context in Taiwan, for example director,

[1] The introduction of this piece in Chinese in PAR. http://par.npac-ntch.org/article/show/1414999923366375.

playwright, and actor Pao-Chang Tsai's creative provocative musicals—such as *Mulan* (2011) on the gender issue—and Jolin and Pao's *PK* (2015), the multi-art pop music and musical production. The performance review of Hakka musical *Xiangsi Nostalgia* (2016) is the translocal theory case study to be explored in terms of translation effort and local creation.

CHAPTER 9

The musical with singing and dance can be visually spectacular, which strengthens plot, character, thought, diction, and music in musical theater—and in turn tells the story (either original or adaptation) better. Some examples include Taiwan's well-known Godot Theatre's restaging of *Kiss Me Nana* (December 2016, Taipei), adapted from the Broadway Musical *Kiss Me Kate* (the musical adaptation of Shakespeare's *The Taming of the Shrew*). The case study in this chapter is the musical *Mountains and Seas* (premiered 2013, restaged May 2017, Taipei) directed by Liang, Chi-Ming, artistic director of Godot Theatre and a professor at National Normal University. The script is adapted from the play *The Classic of Mountains and Seas* written by 2000 Nobel Prize winner Gao Xing-Jian (1940–).

After writing the brief history of the development of the Chinese musical in China and Taiwan, I analyze, comment on, and argue that the issues of love, sexuality, and wars, aided by spectacle, can be visually represented to be more fascinating, to match (what Aristotle didn't know about) audiences' tastes in today's multimedia high-technology era. I focus on Chinese musicals produced in Taiwan to explore whether artistic and successful works can be achieved by adapting either Western canons or Chinese classics, theoretically, not just through translocality, but also by exploring the motifs of hypermedia, hypertext, and literary studies (e.g. Randell Packer and Ken Jordan's *Multimedia: From Wagner to Virtual Reality*, 2001).

CHAPTER 10

As a tribute to the telescope in film director Alfred Hitchcock's *Rear Window*, director Hsin-yao Huang and producer-DP Chung Mong-hong, in the black-and-white Golden Horse winning film *The Great Buddha+* (2017), use the car dashboard camera footage to present the voyeurism of the abject in this digital era. In a comparison of the two maids' sadomasochistic ritual ceremony attempt to murder their employer, Madame, in Jean Genet's play *The Maids*, the two nobodies Belly Bottom (played by

Chen Chu-Sheng) and Prickle (played by Chuang Yi-Zeng) in the film *The Great Buddha+* discover the murder crime committed by Pricke's rich boss Huang Chi-Wen (played by Deon Dai) by watching the footage from the dashboard camera. Visual pleasure, scopophilia, and representation of women in the film are all explored. Film techniques are employed to present the oppression from the rich and the powerful, the huge gap between the rich and the poor, and the farce and absurdity of life.

CHAPTER 11

The book goes on to explore the nuance of the thriller film in the theoretical frame of the female gothic gruesome horror. The cunning and the monstrous are shown in the Golden Horse winning film *The Bold, The Corrupt, and The Beautiful* (2017). Control, ambition, desire, and lust eventually destroy Madame Tang's relationships with her own family, leading to a social realism tragedy. The theme of this film is the ugliness of the human heart, which is even more terrible than ghosts and darker than the corruption of politics. The ten female characters in this film are cunning and the three protagonists in the Tang family are calculating, manipulative, and monstrous. This film can also be viewed as demonstrating, in the words of Ellen Moers (1982), the "abnormal, or monstrous, manifestations of the child–parent tie" (p. 87) in *The Endurance of Frankenstein: Essays on Mary Shelley's Novel* edited by George Levine, and, in so doing, can transform the standard patriarchal family into one of hatred, without love. Since Taiwanese New Cinema was developed in the 1980s, I think that not only is there Bildungsroman narrative expression in this film, but also the identification switch from China to Taiwan. Commentary on the film techniques and reviews are offered in order to appreciate this complex film.

BIBLIOGRAPHY

Moers, Ellen. 1982. "Female Gothic." *The Endurance of Frankenstein: Essays on Mary Shelley's Novel.* Eds. George Levine and U.C. Knoepflmacher. California: University of California Press

Moers, Ellen. "Female Gothic." from Literary Women. The Endurance of Frankenstein: Essays on Mary Shelley's Novel. Ed. George Levine. California: University of California Press, 1982.

CHAPTER 2

Methodologies: From Postcolonial Feminism and Creolization Toward Translocal

Abstract Martin Albrow says Arjun Appadurai is an "advocate for a new postnational discourse and an anthropology that captures the qualities of translocal culture" (p. 1411). In glocalization, imbued with translocal culture, I experience cultural mobility as a scholar travelling across the continents, doing transnational Asian theater and film studies. Appadurai's concept of diaspora and scapes contributes to the creation of translocal theory. Una Chaudhuri's notion of geopathology "in translocal social action" (Fuchs and Chaudhuri, *Land/Scape/Theater*, The University of Michigan Press, 2002, p. 8) also links scape and land in relation to theater and film. Aihwa Ong proposes "Chinese Transnationalism as an Alternative Modernity" (p. 12). The chapter looks at postcolonial history, applying feminism, interculturalism, theories of creolization, postmodernism, and translocality to explore the nuances and complexity of those theater performance cases and film examples.

Keywords Postcolonialism · Feminism · Translocal · Modernities · Transnational

© The Author(s) 2018
I. H. Tuan, *Translocal Performance in Asian Theatre and Film*,
https://Doi.org/10.1007/978-981-10-8609-0_2

According to Martin Albrow, Arjun Appadurai is an "advocate for a new postnational discourse and an anthropology that captures the qualities of translocal culture" (p. 1411).[1] In glocalization, imbued with translocal culture, I find cultural mobility as a scholar travelling across the continents, doing transnational Asian performance and film studies. Arjun Appadurai's concept of diaspora and scapes contributes to the creation of translocal theory. Una Chaudhuri's notion of geopathology "in translocal social action" (Fuchs and Chaudhuri 2002, p. 8) similarly links scape and land in relation to theater.

Asian theater and Asian film are like twins, one in theater performance studies and the other in the film cinema studies, both in Asia. Chinese modernities, in terms of the translocal, can be explored in avant-garde Asian diaspora and transnational relocation. In *Ungrounded Empires*, edited by Aihwa Ong and Donald M. Nolili 1997, their chapter on "Chinese Transnationalism as an Alternative Modernity" try to associate the "Chinese transnational experience as an alternative to modernity" (p. 12) (Martin Albrow's book review p. 1451). Chinese modernities can be achieved through translocal experiences. In transnational capitalism, Asian theater and Asian film, while originally imagined as the Other in world theater and film history, can be mobilized through media studies. Cosmopolitanism can play on while, in this book, we conceptualize the nature of Taiwanese, Chinese, and Asian modernity in those major cities such as Taipei, Hong Kong, Tokyo, Beijing, Shanghai, and in India where transnational Asian theatrical avant-garde productions are staged from postcolonial history to postmodern translocally.

The emergence of transnational capitalism has extended to Asian regional economies, where transnational and multicultural entrepreneurs invest prominently. While this should not deflate the importance of the translocal phenomenon, it should remind us how we are embedded in the world and the discourses within which we convey the translocal Asian performance histories.

Responses are embedded in translocal movements across place, time, and people in dynamic cultural flows. I examine Asian performance and Asian film by using Western methodology. According to Carmen Medina in "'Reading across Communities' in Biliterary Practices: Examining Translocal Discourses and Cultural Flows in Literature Discussions," the theory of translocal can refer to "cultural movements from anthropology

---

[1] In the *American Journal of Sociology*, Martin Albrow in the book review section comments on *Modernity at Large: Cultural Dimensions of Globalization* by Arjun Appadurai.

and cultural studies (Appadurai 1996)" (Medina 2010, p. 40). Moreover, I think the theory of translocalaity can be traced back to the postcolonial theories of cultural flows (Bhabha 1994; Hall 2016), and influential works in Orientalism and Postcolonialism (Said 1994; Fanon 2008), and discourse analysis (Johnstone 2008). Translocality is employed in the cultural production of theater performances and films, particularly transnational, experimental, and avant-garde. This collection of theories serves as useful methodologies for exploring the meanings of transnational Asian theater performances and Asian films.

Translocality is full of cultural dynamic flow. As Medina indicates, it has "dynamically demonstrated the transformative nature of culture across time, space and places." (2010, p. 57). Mobility and multiplicity were complicated in the analysis of cultural production where meanings and symbols are circulated in various contexts to transcend arbitrary cultural attributes, social construction, and fixed locations.

New thinking on the translocal helps broaden our theoretical and spatial understanding of transnational Asian performances and films, and elaborate our expressions of interpreting the meanings of the performances.

Theories like psychoanalysis, postcolonialism, creolization of theory, and feminism can serve as approaches to interpreting the performances. Looking at things from both perspectives (Taiwan/homeland) can be the starting point to initiate our conversation and further discussion in this book.

Brecht's "The Epic Theatre" and "The Alienation Effect" and Artaud's "The Theatre of Cruelty" and *The Theatre and Its Double* still have a huge impact on theater practices and theories nowadays.[2] Literary theories are changing from the traditional dominant position. In *The Creolization of Theory*, for example, Shu-Mei Shih and Françoise Lionnet point out that theories are minorities in the contemporary literature field. However, theory can work well as methodology to frame the scholarly narrative structure. A new theory of the translocal emerges after globalization as a perceived positive optimistic methodology to get us out of the conundrum of abstract philosophical notions. As the past classical literary

---

[2] At Harvard University, thanks go to auditing Professor Homi Bhabha's graduate seminar on Literary Theories (Fall Semester 2012), Professor Marjorie Garber's Shakespeare course (Fall Semester 2012), and Professor Elaine Scarry's course on Political Theatre and the Structure of Drama (Spring Semester 2013). I learned a lot from them when I was a Visiting Scholar doing research there for a year.

theories did, translocality further explains current cultural, social, political, and economical phenomena of mobilities reflected in interdisciplinary anthropology, sociology, ethnography, geography, development studies, and cultural studies. In this new emerging perspective of translocality, I develop the interpretations in Asian theater performance and films.

Figures of Interculturalism

Translocality helps us understand these critiques on interculturalism. Although without as many pluralities as feminism, interculturalism, as discussed by Patrice Pavis, Richard Schechner, Erika Fischer-Lichte, Carol Sorgenfrei, Phillip B. Zarrilli, Rustom Bharucha, and so on, coincided with multiculturalism, intraculturalism, and transculturalism, is still established as a popular practical and useful theoretical methodology.[3]

The Combined Theories Influence the Translocal

Perhaps to better appreciate the works of transnational Asian performance and film over the years, we might substitute the time frame of evolution with the ideas of transnational, intercultural, "in-betweenness," hybridity, creolization, and translocality. The notion of time, translocality, and transnational Asian identity is gradually expanding the boundary through convenient travel and public transportation, enabling the transit of Asian performance from Asia to the US, Europe, and other nations throughout the world. Psychoanalysis such as the ideas of Freud and Lacan, I think, can explain the psychological state of the translocal subjects. Feminism can interpret the pursuit for equality. Interculturalism can dig out the cultural interaction. Postcolonialism and postmodernism can analyze the power in so many post-situations.

In terms of the notion of translocality, the book *Translocality: The Study of Globalizing Processes from a Southern Perspective*, edited by Ulrike

---

[3] See Iris Hsin-chun Tuan. *Intercultural Theatre: Adaptation and Representation*. Germany: Lambert Academic Publishing, 2009. Intercultural Performances can be associated with Peter Brook, Eugenio Barba, and Adriane Mnouchkine, Jerzy Grotowski, Eugenio Barba, Julie Taymor, Emig or Pinder, Robert Lepage, Lee Breuer, Elisabeth LeCompte, John Jesurun, Winston Tong, and Hou Hsiao-Hsien, in music including Philip Glass, David Byrne, Bob Telson, John Cage, and so on. Although, in intercultural and transnational trends, the productions of Robert Wilson and Suzuki Tadashi on cultural hybridity belong more to cultural collage.

Freitag and Achim von Oppen (2010), discusses globalizing processes from the perspective of the humanities and social sciences.[4] According to Freitag and Oppen, translocality seeks to "overcome the main traps of the 'globalization' paradigm, such as its occidental bias, its notion of linear expansion, its simplifying dichotomy between 'local' and 'global,' and an often-found lack of historical depth. They elaborate the asymmetries, mobilities, opportunities and barriers involved in globalizing processes. The concept of 'translocality' aims at integrating a variety of theoretical and methodological approaches from different disciplines." These authors integrate some theories with the emerging discourse on the translocal as the methodological approach to interpreting the issues of time, translocality, and transnational Asian identity in theater, dance, and films in Asia.

The theory of creolization in globalization and transnationalism has scope for translocality to present hybrids of transnational performance studies. I argue that the emergence of transnational theatrical hybrids reflects diverse memory, aesthetic, and mobility practices. Absorbing the legacies of feminism in gender and sex, postcolonialism (postcoloniality) in race, class and power, and performance studies in magnitudes and characters,[5] the interdisciplinary theory of translocality can advance as a new methodology for interpreting the phenomenon after postmodernism about the ongoing avant-garde theater, experimental theater, and postdramatic theater in space and locations. Taking insight from transnationalism, translocality inspires us to think of the dynamics of mobility, migration, and socio-spatial interconnectedness being practiced in Asian theater performances and films.

Let us explore the issues of race, ethnicity, adaptation, and performance in Asian Theater and Asian Film with the methodology of related literary theories. To scrutinize the performance, the actors' performing methods, deconstruction, adaptation, or innovation of the experimental theater forms is implored. Psychoanalysis can be used to decode theater language.

---

[4] Freitag and Oppen's edited book focuses on the "global south," notably the Middle East, Asia, and Africa, while this book focuses on the cases in Asia and North America in order to explore the transAsian American transnational avant-garde performances.

[5] For example, for some related ideas, check Richard Schechner's "Magnitudes of Performance" and Phillip Zarrilli's "What does it mean to 'become the character': power, presence, and transcendence in Asian in-body disciplines of practice" in *By Means of Performance*. Eds. Richard Schechner and Willa Appel. New York: Cambridge University Press, 1997, pp. 19–49, 131–148.

The sub-context of theater language is expressed through Freud's notion of the imaginary. Performers' role-playing is in line with Lacan's mirror stage of identification. Actors' body language on stage consciously, or sometimes unconsciously, expresses the deeper meanings beneath the surface dialogue, as explained by the Iceberg Theory in Psychoanalysis. Lacan's Semiotics is beneficial in decoding the signified; using the theater props and the setting as the signifiers works for the signification of the play. Although sometimes, unfortunately, the reinterpretation of meanings signified and decoded during the process of translation is lost when trying to speak of desire and *jouissance*, sexual pleasure.

Moreover, the cultural, social, and political significance is scrutinized by interculturalism. Patrice Pavis, in *Intercultural Performance Reader*, uses the hourglass as a metaphor to discuss the transfer of meaning from different source culture to the target culture (2001, p. 219).[6]

To connect performance and translocality, I agree with Kanta Kochhar-Lindgren's phrase "translocal performativity." Translocality works not from the opposition tension of the local versus the global, but in the reciprocal change relation. To examine the performance narratives, think of theater as a cultural form and its impact and reflection on contemporary world experiences, and factor in globalization. The agendas include intercultural, transnational, race, gender, cross-boundary, and interdisciplinary questions, so that we can respond to the translocal cultural mobilities.

Bibliography

Albrow, Martin. 1988. Book Review. *American Journal of Sociology*. Vol. 103, No. 5 (March), p. 1411.

Appadurai, Arjun. 1996. *Modernity at Large: Cultural Dimensions of Globalization*. Minneapolis & London: University of Minnesota Press.

Benjamin, Walter. 1936. *Illuminations*. 1969[1936], p. 218, pp. 220–221. "The work of Art in the Age of Mechanical Reproduction." Source: UCLA School of Theater, Film and Television; Translated: by Harry Zohn; Published: by Schocken/Random House, ed. by Hannah Arendt; Transcribed: by Andy Blunden 1998; proofed and corrected Feb. 2005. https://www.marxists.org/reference/subject/philosophy/works/ge/benjamin.htm.

Bhabha, Homi. 1994. The Location of Culture. London and New York: Routledge.

---

[6] Patrice Pavis. *Theatre at the Crossroads of Culture*. London and New York: Routledge, 2001.

Cheng Fan-Ting. 2013. "Dreamers' Nightmare: The Melancholia of the TaiwaneseCentennial Celebration." *Asian Theatre Journal*. Vol. 30 no.1: Spring, pp. 172–188.

Diamond, Catherine. 1994. "*Kingdom of Desire*: The Three Faces of *Macbeth*." *Asia Theatre Journal* 11, no. 1: 114–133.

———. 1995. "Reflected and Refracted: Metatheatrics in Taiwan." *Journal of Dramatic Theory and Criticism*. vol. 9, no. 2: 84–96.

Fanon, Frantz. 2008. Black Skin, White Masks. Translation by Richard Philcox. New York: Grove Press.

Felluga, Dino. 2012. "Modules on Baudrillard: On Simulation." *Introductory Guide to Critical Theory*. Purdue U. Access Date: April 2, 2016. https://www.cla.purdue.edu/english/theory/postmodernism/modules/baudlldsimulTnmainframe.html.

Foley, Kathy. 2016. "Book Review." *Modern Asian Theatre and Performance 1900–2000*. Kevin J. Wetmore Jr., Siyuan Liu, and Erin B. Mee. The Modern Drama Anthology of Modern Plays. Eds. Siyuan Liu and Kevin J. Wetmore Jr. *Asian Theatre Journal*. 33, no. 1: 217–220.

Freitag, Ulrike. & Oppen, von Achim. 2010. Translocality: The Study of Globalising Processes from a Southern Perspective. Leidon and Boston: Brill.

Fuchs, Elinor & Chaudhuri, Una. 2002. *Land/Scape/Theater*. Ann Arbor: The University of Michigan Press.

Hall, Stuart. 2016. Cultural Studies 1983: A Historical History. (Stuart Hall Selected Writing). Eds. Jennifer Daryl Slack and Lawrence Grossberg. Durham and London: Duke University Press.

Johnstone, Barbara. 2008. Discourse Analysis. Malden and Oxford: Blackwell Publishing.

Medina, Carmen. 2010. "Reading across Communities in Biliteracy Practices: Examing Translocal Discourse and Cultural Flows in Literature Discussions." Reading Research Quarterly. Vol. 45. No. 1. (Jan.–March), pp. 40–60.

Ong, Aihwa & Nonini, Donald. 1997. Eds. Ungrounded Empires. New York: Routledge.

Patrice Pavis. 2001. Theatre at the Crossroads of Culture. London and New York: Routledge.

Said, Edward. 1994. Orientalism. New York: Random House.

PART I

Intercultural Theatre in Taiwan

CHAPTER 3

Contemporary Legend Theatre's *A Midsummer Night's Dream*: Tradition, Modernity, and Translocality

Abstract Shakespeare's *A Midsummer Night's Dream* produced by the Contemporary Legend Theatre (CLT) in Taipei in March 2016, starring actor Wu Hsing-kuo and actress Wei Hai-Min, was intended to interpret the Bard in terms of Asian intercultural Shakespearean performance. The tradition upheld in Chinese Peking Opera has often undergone innovations in modernity. In diasporic hybridity, one feels, tradition and modernity blend the synchronic and diachronic relationships of human beings and places. The transboundary images in the local Taiwan performance complement the global Shakespearean idiom. The binary opposition between the specific and the universal gradually disappear in the contemporary translocal parlance. It is argued that this live performance, after the script adaptation and theater representation in cross-country and cross-racial terms, displays the Asian dream and local cultural imagination.

Keywords Contemporary Legend Theatre (CLT) • *A Midsummer Night's Dream* • Modernity • Asian intercultural Shakespearean performance • Chinese Peking Opera

© The Author(s) 2018
I. H. Tuan, *Translocal Performance in Asian Theatre and Film*,
https://doi.org/10.1007/978-981-10-8609-0_3

Tradition of Shakespeare's Legacy and Chinese Peking Opera

This chapter explores the premiere of *A Midsummer Night's Dream* in Taipei in March 2016 by the Contemporary Legend Theatre (CLT), and touches upon the issues of tradition and modernity in Asian intercultural Shakespearean performance, specifically in relation to Taiwan, through the perspective of translocality. From the lovers' romantic hallucinations in Shakespeare's *A Midsummer Night's Dream* to the slogan of the Sixth International Theatre Olympics in Beijing ("China's dream meets the world's stage", Kim 2016, p. 199), the theaters in Taiwan also combined tradition and modernity in Oriental/Occidental terms to realize their ongoing dreams of innovation.

To celebrate the 400th anniversary of Shakespeare's death, Taiwan, as well as the UK, paid tribute to the Bard. The CLT's *A Midsummer Night's Dream* highlighted issues of tradition and modernity in Taiwan's intercultural Shakespeare from the perspective of translocality. This production supports ideas advanced by Huang in *Chinese Shakespeares* (2009) challenging the fidelity, authenticity, and cultural exclusivity of Shakespeare as being confined to Anglophone Shakespeares.

In the wake of cultural diffusion, Shakespeare and his works are part of the UK's cultural heritage, incarnate as the iconic brand—through glocalization, re-visualized in ways that produce modernity from tradition in globalization. The CLT's *A Midsummer Night's Dream* followed Shakespeare's plot and was performed mainly in Chinese, but with some monologues in English, and a little Taiwanese and Japanese. The production used fashionable, contemporary costumes. More traditional *jingju* singing was mixed with Broadway-esque tunes. The overall effect represented modernity. The free adaptation of traditional elements in this piece resembled what one might expect of Yukio Ninagawa, Ariane Mnouchkine, or Ong Keng Sen. The production provided interesting take on the fairy world, but was not without its weaknesses.

Traditional theater formats in Taiwan include Peking opera, *kunju*, *yueju*, Taiwanese opera, and puppet theater, among others. Some noteworthy intercultural Shakespearean performances have achieved fusion with Asian elements—such as Japanese director Yukio Ninagawa's *Macbeth* and *Hamlet*; French director Ariane Mnouchkine's adaptation of *Richard II* in Japanese style; and Singaporean director Ong Keng Sen's *Desdemona*. Modern theaters in Taiwan have thus staged many Asian-Shakespearean theater art works.

*And as imagination bodies forth
The forms of things unknown, the poet's pen
Turns them to shapes and gives to airy nothing
A local habitation and a name.*
(William Shakespeare, *A Midsummer Night's Dream*, V. i.)[1]

Imagination is not just fantasized and fabricated by the poet's pen. In globalization, the inspiration of the classics can manifest under different names.
From local to global, here and now in a slipstream of dream and imagination, what Shakespeare wrote in the court scene in *A Midsummer Night's Dream*, still rings true:

Hippolyta:
'Tis strange my Theseus, that these lovers speak of.
Theseus:
More strange than true: I never may believe
These antique fables, nor these fairy toys.
Lovers and madmen have such seething brains,
Such shaping fantasies, that apprehend
More than cool reason ever comprehends.

(Act V Scene 1)

Lovers, madmen, and poets have the unique imagination to be able to turn the insubstantial into living paradigms. In various forms, through adaptation, deconstruction, and representation, nurturing innovative modernity out of tradition to be reborn anew.

HISTORY OF MODERN ASIAN SHAKESPEARE PERFORMANCES IN TAIWAN

As Kathy Foley observes in her book review of *Modern Asian Theatre and Performance 1900–2000*, written by Kevin J. Wetmore Jr., Siyuan Liu, and Erin B. Mee, the authors' contention is "(t)o understand modern Asian theatre is to understand modern Asian society" (p. 13). Foley observes

---

[1] I am grateful to the English-language writer Associate Professor Rupendra Guha Majumdar, a Fulbright Scholar, working at the Department of English, University of Delhi, whose expertise in American Literature and Drama, who helped edit this chapter draft in the preliminary stage.

that the "opening discussion sees modernity and modern drama in Asia as interlinked" (2016, p. 218). Asian Shakespeare performances in Taiwan largely began in the 1980s in college theater performance competitions and the developing little theater movement (see Tuan 2007). The tertiary level students either translated works into Chinese or performed Shakespeare in English in these competitions or for performances in their departments of English or Foreign Languages and Literatures. Though the first efforts may have been amateur, things changed with time.

Some professional theater companies have staged Asian Shakespeare performances in Taiwan, such as the CLT (1986–), Ping-Fong Acting Group (1986–2014), Godot Theatre Company (1988–), Tainaner Ensemble (1987–), and so on. For example, Lee Kuo-hsiu (Hugh K. S. Lee, 1955–2013) and his company Pingfeng Acting Troupe (Pingfeng Biaoyan Ban), staged the successful production *Shamlet* (1986–2014, a deconstructed *Hamlet*). This play, which has been discussed by Huang (2005) and Diamond (1995), is a farce, with the structure of a play-within-a-play, about a mediocre touring troupe staging *Hamlet*, advertised as *Shamlet* due to the troupe's printing error. *Shamlet* was "filled with technical and performance blunders, backstage intrigues and stabbings behind each other's backs. In a way, the play provides a mirror to the mixed qualities of burgeoning theatrical companies since the 1980s" (Liu in Wetmore et al. 2014, p. 132). *Shamlet* helped lead the way in localizing Shakespeare. Soon, professional theater companies were staging Shakespearean performances: these included CLT's *Kingdom of Desire* (1986, from *Macbeth*), *War and Eternity* (1990, from *Hamlet*), *Lear Is Here* (2000, an offshoot of *King Lear*), and *The Tempest* (2004); Godot Theatre Company's *Othello* (2008) and *Kiss Me Kate* (1997, the musical based on *The Taming of the Shrew*), and *New Taming of the Shrew* (1994); and Tainaner Ensemble's *Witches' Sonata—Macbeth Poetry* (2003) and two works inspired by *Romeo and Juliet*, *Shakespeare Unplugged—Romeo and Juliet* (2004) and *K24-Chaoes* (2005). Taiwanese theater companies—such as Stan Lai's Performance Workshop (with works like *Lear and the 37fold Path of a Bodhisattva*, 2000), Wu Hsing-kuo's CLT, and Liang Chi-Ming's Godot Theatre—have performed their Shakespearean works in Taiwan and toured internationally, often enthusiastically received by audiences.

In *Modern Asian Theatre and Performance 1900–2000*, as Wetmore et al. report: "Modern spoken theatre in Taiwan and Hong Kong are inexorably linked to *huaju* (spoken drama) in mainland China, because they have emerged from the same roots and have continued to interact with each other, particularly since the 1980s" (2014, p. 125). As for theater history in Taiwan, according to Liu:

> spoken theatre in Taiwan has been closely tied to its tumultuous history in the twentieth century. The island was ceded to Japan in 1895 as a result of China's defeat in the Sino-Japanese War (1894–1895) and remained under Japanese control until 1945. In 1949, the nationalist government lost the civil war in mainland China, retreated to Taiwan and declared martial law, which remained in effect until 1987. (Wetmore et al. 2014, pp. 125–126)

In the late 1920s, the spoken theater productions were known as *"xinju* (new drama) or *wenhuaju* (cultural drama), as they were staged by socalled 'cultural societies.' They were heavily influenced by Japanese *shingeki* (new drama) and Chinese *wenmingxi* (civilized drama) and *huaju"* (Wetmore et al. 2014, p. 126). Now, as mentioned earlier, audiences in China and overseas locations have enthusiastically received performances from Taiwan theater companies.

Notwithstanding inconsistent government support of large-scale, commercial theaters or independent theaters, Asian Shakespeare performances have, more or less, taken place in Taiwan. For example, Hugh K. S. Lee, a veteran of Lanling Theatre and Performance Group, created his own company The Pingfeng Acting Troupe (Pingfeng Biaoyan Ban), and staged the successful production *Shamlet*. As Catherine Diamond observes: "*Shamlet* is uniquely Taiwanese, and therefore reflects not only Taiwanese theatrical conditions, but the society as well ... a response ... to the selfish materialism of contemporary Taiwan society which threatens to subvert the collaboration necessary for theatrical performance" (1995, p. 94).

With *Shamlet*, Lee tackled self-parody, a personal story of running the troupe in crisis, plots of marriage and various urban affairs, and the proverbial conflict between artistic ideals and commercial entertainment.

"Loosely based on Michael Frayn's *Noises Off* and elements of Mel Brook's film *To Be or Not to Be*," for Siyuan Liu, *Shamlet* is "filled with technical and performance blunders, backstage intrigues and stabbings behind each other's backs. In a way, the play provides a mirror to the mixed qualities of burgeoning theatrical companies since the 1980s" (Wetmore et al. 2014, p. 132). In my view, *Shamlet* is a milestone in Taiwan local theater companies' capability to stage their own Asian Shakespeare creation.

Therefore, I argue that the live performance of CLT's *A Midsummer Night's Dream*, following the script adaptation, displays the Asian dream and the indigenous cultural imagination. Cultural mobility under globalization interacts with the imaginative community in the hybrid discourse of online websites and the real theater space. All of the images, media, information, and performances manifest Shakespeare's influence and Chinese Peking opera as intangible cultural heritage to represent not just tradition but also modernity.

CLT's *A Midsummer Night's Dream*

Facing the decline of *jingju* in Taiwan and with only a few old and loyal audience members, CLT has since the 1980s sought to regenerate the tradition by imbuing it with modern elements (See Huang 2009; Diamond 1994). As Catherine Diamond points out, the performers "were concerned because Peking Opera was not only losing its present audience of elderly knowledgeable supporters but failing to attract replacements; without an audience appreciative of the subtleties of the form, it would gradually disappear" (1994, p. 114). CLT's *A Midsummer Night's Dream* (Fig. 3.1)

Fig. 3.1 Cast and the team group photo. CLT's *A Midsummer Night's Dream* (March 2016, National Theater in Taipei). (Courtesy of CLT)

was a Taiwanese dream and showed local cultural imagination: the images, media, and performance embody both *xiqu* and Shakespeare, allowing the intangible cultural heritage of *jingju* to coincide in a work of modernity.

Adapting Shakespeare's early comedy, *A Midsummer Night's Dream*, Wu Hsing-kuo, as artistic director of the company and its lead actor, used a script adaptation written by the well-known Chinese novelist Chang Ta-chuen, with some of the original (English) speeches. Wu Hsing-kuo played Oberon/Theseus and the female lead Wei Hai-min, Titania/Hippolyta. However, with much of the appeal being the character of Puck—Fairy King Oberon's capable sprite—promotion and public relations were focused around him. CLT's producer Lin Hsiu-Wei sold the production to youth as being "rock and roll *jingju*" and "fashion musical" (composed by Wang Hsi-Wen), as reported in the *ETToday* newspaper by Tsai. But, Associate Professor Zhang Xiao-xiong (2016) at Taipei National University of the Arts called it: "Tone deaf, eastern & western hodgepodge, ridiculous, intolerable to the ear". While the promotional material seemed to promise a Broadway Musical, this was not the reality. This was *jingju* with modern hybrid characteristics. Cirque du Soleil acrobatics and contemporary popular music were added to attract young audiences to come along with Shakespeare lovers to buy tickets for a twenty-first century *jingju*.

Since the success of *The Kingdom of Desire* in 1986, Wu has continued to wave the banner of rejuvenating traditional Peking opera by mixing *jingju* with Western scripts, seeking to attract youthful viewers. Producer Lin Hsiu-Wei also adds some elements, like that of the "rock and roll Peking opera" and the "fashion Peking opera." CLT boasts about incorporating Broadway musical items in this particular Peking opera performance. However, firstly, it would be honest to say that CLT's *A Midsummer Night's Dream* is not like a Broadway musical at all, but rather a poor imitation. The artistic contribution of Broadway and European musicals with scores, music, melody, and lyrics from Jerome Kern, Rodgers and Hammerstein, Stephen Sondheim, Andrew Lloyd Webber, and so on, is so much more than what this performance boldly claims to be. It is not a good thing for CLT to make a great whoop and holler about their attempt to stage a "Broadway musical-like Peking Opera," because, after all, it is simply not so.

In the CLT performance of *A Midsummer Night's Dream* Puck flew through the air on long swathes of cloth, performing graceful poses inspired by the moves that Taiwanese dancer Billy Chang Yi-Chun had mastered in his role as Fire in Cirque du Soleil's *Dralion*. Chang became a Taiwanese icon through his participation in Cirque and was a graceful Puck. He tried to be center stage. Billy Chang's Puck is vigorous; he wears skin color tights decorated with shining crystals, one naked leg exposing muscle and his masculinity. Chang's aerial acrobatics as Puck created a powerful and athletic fairy world. He showed upper body strength, strong spatial orientation, and his circus roots were clear. He also performed on the ground. He demonstrated his speed by inline roller skating, symbolizing flashing around the world in the twinkling of an eye to fetch the flowers ordered by the brooding King Oberon. His inline roller skating showed off his swift speed after stating "I'll put a girdle round about the earth/In forty minutes" (II, ii, l. 178–179).

He likewise mounted a skateboard to demonstrate his dexterity and mischievous character. Chang's movement is commendable; however, the artistic mastery and precision of execution in roller skating skills and skateboard techniques could have definitely been improved. His skating techniques, while speedy, were not fully developed as dance; more hand gestures and full body choreography might have merited greater applause. For instance, he might have added more figure skating techniques, such as jumps, spins, and steps, to his repertoire, in order to increase audience appreciation.

Chang's interaction with the front rows during the intermission proved tedious. His nonsensical screams seemed more like harsh noise than the sounds of the fairy world. Eventually, with this production still on tour, performances in different cities in Taiwan and probably overseas in the future, we can expect to see a superb artist playing the role of Puck, also known as "Robin Goodfellow" (II. i.). As Puck says in Shakespeare's text:

> I am that merry wanderer of the night.
> I jest to Oberon and make him smile. (II. i.)

We, the audience members, as well as Oberon, would like to be consistently amused by the antics of the immaculate Puck.

The lovers (Kung Yueh-tzu's Hermia, Chu Bo-chen's Lysander, Huang Jo-lin's Helena, and Huang Ching-tang's Demetrius), lacking profound *jingju* foundation, did not impress. They attempted to insert *xiqu*, especially in the fighting scene, and even called each other by their real names. However, it was inappropriate for the women to strip to white underwear considering their given statuses in the script and in *jingju*. Lysander and

Demetrius lacked deep characterization and were interchangeable. The mechanicals, however, did well with farce: Pyramus and Thisbe used semi-*kabuki* style to create merriment. The four minor fairy roles mixed ballet, modern dance, pop jazz dance, and hip hop to create beautiful movement in the fairy world.

The last scene (V. i.) in the play where the Fairy King Oberon and the Fairy Queen Titania lead the fairies to the court to bless the just-married couples (V. i. p. 246) is necessarily omitted. The reason is that Actor Wu and Actress Wei both play the two main roles—Wu plays that of Theseus and Oberon, and Wei that of Hippolyta and Titania, thus making it impossible for them to appear simultaneously in the double roles.

In the notes from the director "Future Sparkles from Conflicts" in the program, Wu compares them to the Troupe Members (Tailor, Mason, Cook, Carpenter, and Blacksmith) in the play within the-play to express his opinion: "Allow me to borrow Shakespeare's words to end this brief article."

> The lunatic, the lover and the poet
> Are of imagination all compact: (V, i, 7–8)

As mentioned already, Wu and Wei played Theseus and Hippolyta as well as the fairy monarchs, meaning the blessing scene at the end of the play had to be left out. Speaking for the troupe, Wu as Theseus delivered the lines Shakespeare gave to Puck:

> If we shadows have offended,
> Think but this, and all is mended,
> That you have but slumb'red here
> While these visions did appear. (V, i, 423–426)

As Wu's (2016, p. 15) notes in the program remind us: "We are but a hardworking troupe, sincerely and diligently staging a comedy to entertain both the audience and ourselves. ... See you next time in theatre!" (Program 2016, p. 15).

The big difference in this performance (performed mainly in Mandarin) is that both Billy Chang's Puck and Wu Hsing-kuo's Theseus deliver parts of their monologues using Shakespeare's original words in English.

Reception

But there were shortcomings. To fulfill the dream of *jingju* Shakespearean performance, a solid foundation of performing skills are more needed than the eye-catching special effects, fashionable costumes, and exaggerated PR. This production did not live up to CLT's previous successes in mounting Shakespeare. Professor Shih Kuang-Sen of National Taiwan University of Arts (NTUA) evaluates this performance as poor, at least, not good enough; and the singing is regarded as especially unsatisfactory. Professor Kuo Chiang-sheng (2016) of Donghwa University found it to be a fiasco noting that, "Shakespeare's Comedy [became] Wu Hsing-kuo's Tragedy." Wu was weak not just in traditional *jingju* singing, but also in his Broadway musical style songs, despite being trained by *jingju* Master Chou Cheng-Jung (周正榮, 1925–2000), who was publicly recognized as one of the great four who excelled in performing the old man role (*lao shen*, 老生) in Taiwan. The experts, critics, and connoisseurs in Taiwan criticize Wu for his poor voice and terrible singing. NTU Professor Wang An-Chi, for example, comments on Wu's failure in restaging Master Chou's representative traditional Peking opera repertory 《問樵鬧府; for the fact is that Wu started from his profession as a *Wuseng* (武生), a male warrior role in Peking opera.

However, although Wu has often been faulted for his weakness in singing and command of various role types, Professor Wang An-chi (2003) feels Wu's initial training in a martial (*wu*) role limits his range. Some have urged Wu to improve his voice or bring in someone who can sing for or with him. Even the female lead, Wei, who is known for her musicality, failed to gain praise in this "fashionable *jingju*." The Broadway style songs did not work. Ultimately, lacking the musical expertise, this production was bad *jingju* and bad Broadway (Fig. 3.2). Her previous performances, like her collaboration with American director Robert Wilson to perform the solo *Orlando* in 2009 at the National Theater in Taipei, were far better acclaimed. The latter outcome was, in fact, neither fish nor fowl, neither traditional Peking opera nor Broadway musical. The audience response to her singing the new Broadway musical style songs was low key. What a plight it was to see the famous local *jingju* stars fail in this Asian-Shakespearean adaptation comedy!

This performance of CLT's *A Midsummer Night's Dream* has not developed into a satisfactory or well-acclaimed production through its attempt to mix tradition and modernity, so far. It was faulted on *jingju* singing, acting, and stylization. Its claim of being something equal to a Broadway musical was

Fig. 3.2 Fairy King (played by Wu Hsing-Kuo in golden yellow costume) and Fairy Queen (played by Wei Hai-Min in silver white costume) have a quarrel over the ownership of the cute boy in the forest scene. CLT's *A Midsummer Night's Dream* (March 2016, National Theater in Taipei). (Courtesy of CLT)

not realized. Only Chang Yung-hsuan, a girl who plays the Fairy Boy sang popular songs well and with a clear voice full of innocence. Nevertheless, *A Midsummer Night's Dream* did exemplify the desired translocality—going across the limitation of ethnoscapes and specific local drama types—valued in current Taiwanese Shakespeare. CLT's *A Midsummer Night's Dream* used Shakespeare's play, mixed with the style of the Broadway musical, and broke the boundaries of Chinese theater tradition. the production used Shakespeare's play to reinvent its Taiwanese voice, signaling modernity through script adaptation and *jingju* reworking.

This somewhat problematic production reinforces the historical point of a larger intercultural project of transnational adaptations of Shakespeare as an ongoing process of localization. There is value even in such flawed adaptations, and the critiques of Wu's new attempt can perhaps push him toward a more productive direction. Intercultural Shakespearean performances are found everywhere in Asia and authenticity is a useless term in a time of globalization. What I term translocality in Shakespeare productions prevails in

Taiwan and cultural mobility is normal in theater today. Shakespearean performances are deterritorialized in productions such as *jingju* Shakespeare by CLT, but genres may still exert their demands. Profound singing, reciting, acting, and fighting are requirements of *jingju*. CLT's *A Midsummer Night's Dream* was disappointing to many audience members and critics because of its failure as *jingju*. Ads like "*jingju* with hip hop" or "Broadway musical" are nonsensical if there is little or no *jingju* or the musical model is lacking. We want Wu to rediscover the artistry exhibited, for example, in *Kingdom of Desire* (1986). Intercultural Shakespearean performances can be opened up to the young generation, but the directing choices have to be made with artistic flair and expertise. Half-baked *jingju* and half-baked Shakespeare will not draw new audiences toward either of these iconic genres.

CLT's *A Midsummer Night's Dream* mixes Shakespeare's English play, with snippets of Broadway musical from the US, and Chinese stylization of the Peking opera. For sure, it is an Asian intercultural performance. The notion of time, translocality, and transnational Asian identity under the big umbrella of Asian Shakespeare is gradually breaking the boundaries of the specific national theater tradition. In globalization and glocalization, within a heterogeneous cultural flow, indeed no cultural "authenticity" can be claimed, as Walter Benjamin affirmed in his notion of "aura" in global mechanical and electrical reproduction. Asian intercultural Shakespearean performances, in the stringent context of an English literary tradition, pursue Patrice Pavis' theory of the filter metaphor, to transmit to the target culture in Asia. Moreover, Asian intercultural Shakespearean performances such as CLT's *A Midsummer Night's Dream* transform the traditional literature of Shakespeare's plays into Asian linguistic idiom—from English to Chinese and Taiwanese languages, and culture translocations.

Some people might wonder why I chose the flawed CLT's performance as an example to explain the theme of tradition and modernity. There are at least three reasons. First, referring to the sinking of the Titanic metaphorically: if no one talks about this CLT performance (even if it's not so well acclaimed as their past masterpieces, like *Kingdom of Desire* and *Lear is Here*) it will be just like an untraced ship sailing silently across the broad sea late at night in total darkness, totally unobserved. At least by discussing this premiere performance here I have created a historical document; which will mean the production is remembered and hopefully improved in the future. Secondly, just as Stan Lai's *Dreamers* (the Taiwanese Centennial Celebration Performance) is criticized as being a nightmare because of its huge staging costs and its outdated, nostalgia drenched drama, at least this performance is recorded for posterity, unabashedly. The same goes for Wu's *A Midsummer Night's Dream*. Thirdly, no doubt, CLT is a suitable example to demonstrate roots sprouting from the tradition of Peking opera, and continuous agenda of modernization. Hopefully this critique of Wu's new production can be a useful study of his fallen trajectory in recent years.

In cultural mobility and diasporic hybridity, I think that in-between tradition and modernity people who have a connection to the location experience simultaneous synchronic and diachronic simulation. In particular, the lines between here and there, now and then, reality and simulacra, and the realistic and the fictional landscapes the audiences see are blurred. The flow of people and information are related to translocality. Just as Appadurai visualized, "The many displaced, de-territorialized, and transient populations that constitute today's ethnos capes, are engaged in the construction of locality" (1996, p. 199). Examining the relationship between the dimensions of global cultural flows, further refracting this disjuncture are what Appadurai calls *mediascapes* and *ideoscapes*, "which are closely related landscapes of images" (p. 35). Ideas flow indulgently across landscapes.

Ideas of staging intercultural, Shakespearean performances are flowing in the US, Europe, and Asia. Nowadays it is hard to locate authenticity in globalization. What Walter Benjamin's theoretical concept of "authenticity, presence, and aura" was going toward, but what he did not deal with was "simulation." As Richard Schechner in *Performance Studies* explains: "With simulation representation ends, and reproduction (cloning, digital and biological) takes over" (p. 117). Appadurai in "The Production of Locality" questions the concept: "What is the place of locality in schemes about global cultural flow?" He is also concerned with "what locality might mean in a situation where the nation-state faces particular sorts of transnational destabilization" (p. 178). I try to attempt an answer to this by offering the theory of translocality.

In my opinion, the binary opposition between the specific and the universal is gradually disappearing into translocality. I think theatrical mobility exists in different adaptations, while cultures in translocality and diverse theater performance methods add to glocalization. By glocalization here, I mean the globalization in addition to the local specific cultural flavor concerning cultural mobility. From England in Europe to Taiwan in Asia, cultural currents flow in *A Midsummer Night's Dream*, from the blindness and erratic inconstancy of capricious love to cultural heterogeneity and theatrical hybridity. Nature as a background—the woods in *A Midsummer Night's Dream* or *Macbeth*, the storm-tossed heath in *King Lear*, the forbidden island in *The*

Tempest—reflects human nature: love, madness, revenge, and ambition; and in terms of cultural mobility, cultures in translocality enrich the plentiful and diverse theater performance methods around the world.

Conclusion

CLT's *A Midsummer Night's Dream* can be demonstrated as a good example of an intercultural performance illustrating the notion of translocality. With the prevalence of translocal communication, we are aware of various theater productions with intercultural performative expressions in the twenty-first century. Patrice Pavis' edited anthology, *The Intercultural Performance Reader* (1996), including such viewpoints as that of Rustom Bharucha, was a milestone in critical analysis. To cross territorial boundaries and break through the limitations of the single local culture, some theater institutions, including CLT, have already combined more than two or three different cultural or theatrical forms to stage intercultural performances.

Since historical precedence, locality structured by feeling is owned by social life, including long distance commerce and migrations. Crossing the boundaries of territorial limitation, I think that cultural performances as Asian intercultural Shakespearean performances are deterritorialized; not limited to the types and styles of Peking opera, *kunju*, *yueju*, Japanese *noh* or *kabuki*, Indian *kathakali*, spoken drama, experimental theater, avant-garde theater, and Broadway musical, to name just a few. Instead, we should progress toward the totality of artistic creation. However, no matter how creative we are, innovation still demands the foundation of a sound performance tradition. Modernity like new leaves grows from the tree of tradition.

Just as ethnoscapes are about the construction of locality, the particular stylization of Peking opera, profound artistic singing, reciting, acting, and fighting are its requirements. CLT's *A Midsummer Night's Dream*, despite the despair of many audiences and critics, must still work on the polish and refinement of the core of the artistic expression of Peking opera. Otherwise, all of the other facetious advertisements—like "fashion opera," "rock and roll opera," "Peking opera with hip hop," and "Peking opera in addition to the aura of the Broadway musical"—are a total sham. We expect to see the other milestone, CLT's well-acclaimed *Kingdom of Desire* (1986). Eventually, our dream of making intercultural Asian Shakespeare performances accessible to the young generation and successful enough to attract everyone can come true. That is the agenda worth celebrating together, beyond the 400th anniversary of Shakespeare's death.

BIBLIOGRAPHY

Appadurai, Arjun. 1996. *Modernity at Large: Cultural Dimensions of Globalization.* 1st Edition. Minneapolis and London: University of Minnesota Press.
CLT. 2016. Program of *A Midsummer Night's Dream.* (Fashion Legend Musical.) Taipei: Contemporary Legend Theatre.
Diamond, Catherine. 1994. "*Kingdom of Desire*: The Three Faces of *Macbeth.*" *Asia Theatre Journal* 11, no. 1: 114–133.
———. 1995. "Reflected and Refracted: Metatheatrics in Taiwan." *Journal of Dramatic Theory and Criticism* 9, no. 2: 84–96.
Foley, Kathy. 2016."Book Review." Modern Asian Theatre and Performance 1900–2000. Kevin J. Wetmore Jr., Siyuan Liu, and Erin B. Mee. The Modern Drama Anthology of Modern Plays. Eds. Siyuan Liu and Kevin J. Wetmore Jr. Asian Theatre Journal. 33, no. 1: 217–220.
Kim, Kyoung Jae. 2016. "Performance Review. The Sixth International Theatre Olympics in Beijing." *Asian Theatre Journal*, vol. 33, no. 1: 198–202.
Huang, Alexander [Alexa]. 2005. "Impersonation, Autobiography, and Cross-Cultural Adaptation: *Lee Kuo-Hsiu's Shamlet.*" *Asian Theatre Journal* 22, no. 1: 122–137.
———. 2009. *Chinese Shakespeares: Two Centuries of Cultural Exchange.* New York: Columbia University Press.
Schechner, Richard. 2002. "Simulation, Jean Baudrillard." *Performance Studies: An Introduction.* London and New York: Routledge, pp. 117–122.
Steger, B. Manfred. 2014. "Interview with Appadurai." *Globalizations*, vol. 11 (4): 481–490.
Tuan, Iris Hsin-chun. 2007. *Alternative Theater in Taiwan: Feminist and Intercultural Approaches.* New York: Cambria Press.
Wang, An-Chi. 2003. 《寂寞沙洲冷—周正榮京劇藝術》 ("Lonely Cold Alluvion—Chou Cheng-Jung's Peking Opera Art."), Yilan: National Center for Traditional Arts.
Wetmore, J. Kevin, Liu, Siyuan, and Mee, B. Erin. 2014. *Modern Asian Theatre and Performance 1900–2000.* London and New York.
Wu, Hsing-kuo. 2016. Program of A Midsummer Night's Dream. (Fashion Legend Musical.) Taipei: Contemporary Legend Theatre.

Websites

Kuo, Chiang-sheng. 2016. 《莎翁的喜劇,吳興國的悲劇》 (Shakespeare's Comedy, Wu Hsing-kuo's Tragedy) *ARTalks*, 28 March, http://talks.taishinart.org.tw/juries/kjs/2016032801, accessed 8 June 2016.

Tsai, Shao-chien. 2016. 《京劇基因打造音樂莎劇 當代傳奇譜時尚《仲夏夜之夢》 (*Jingju* Gene Creates Musical Shakespeare. CLT Composes Fashion *A Midsummer Night's Dream*). http://www.ettoday.net/news/20160324/668503.htm, accessed 12 June 2016.

Zhang, Xiao-xiong. 2016. 《饒了莎翁吧!》 (Give Shakespeare a Break). *ARTalks*, 25 March. http://talks.taishinart.org.tw/juries/xxz/2016032501, accessed 12 June 2016.

CHAPTER 4

Yukio Ninagawa's *Hamlet* in Taiwan: Intercultural Representation

Abstract Representing Japan's indelible scenes in the Meiji period stage designed by Setsu Asakura, director Yukio Ninagawa (1935–2016)'s *Hamlet* was performed at the National Theater of Taiwan (premiere March 26, 2015, Taipei). I explore this Japanese flavor and argue both authentic Japanese cultural roots and Western–Asian intercultural impact. In the play-within-the-play-within-the-play, Ninagawa represents the Mouse Trap scene by performing the simulation murder twice—once through mime, and second with *kabuki*. Claudius' confession scene is filled with Japanese sadist torture style. The actress playing Ophelia sings Japanese songs to express her insanity. "Who are you?" is asked in Ninagawa's *Hamlet*. Filtered with Western influence in the last fighting scene, and Japanese target culture as the representation of Fortinbras, this is a fusion of intercultural performance.

Keywords Yukio Ninagawa • *Hamlet* • Representation • Intercultural performance

INTRODUCTION

Intercultural representation was demonstrated when the Japanese director Yukio Ninagawa (1935–2016)[1] was invited to stage *Hamlet*, adapted from Shakespeare's play (premiere March 26, 2015, Taipei), at the National Theater in Taiwan before touring in the UK in Europe. Bringing a Shakespearean play that has originated in England and been adapted to an Asian foreign form back to its birth place, suggests that Western cultural imperialism and colonialism can be balanced by the Far Eastern intercultural performance forms, in order to share Shakespeare's universality as a global cultural legacy.[2] Is Ninagawa's *Hamlet* (2015, Taipei) a Japanese Shakespearean performance digging out Shakespeare's roots or a Shakespeare's play performed in Japanese, just adding a little Japanese exotic flavor? Ninagawa, in the performance program, said he would like to present "not simply a *Hamlet* with a little Japanese flavor like a souvenir you bring home from the trips abroad, but instead looking into its roots, not its leaves" (2015, p. 4). However, according to Yong Li Lan in "Shakespeare and the fiction of the Intercultural" in *A Companion to Shakespeare and Performance*, "Ninagawa's intercultural strategies have often been criticized as a Japanese styling and exoticism targeted at Western or global festival consumption" (p. 543). In this chapter, I explore these complex issues of Ninagawa's *Hamlet* (2015, Taipei) through intercultural theater representation and the audience reception in Taiwan.

---

[1] Ninagawa Yukio's biography and his directing productions touring abroad in Europe, the US and Asia can be checked in Wikipedia and the official website of Ninagawa Troupe, such as Yukio Ninagawa at the Internet Movie Database and NINAGAWA STUDIO WEBSITE.

[2] Some examples of glowing internationalization of Asian Shakespeare since the 1980s are, referring to the initial production; many of those productions have been revived subsequently: "Ninagawa Yukio's productions (*Ninagawa Macbeth*, 1980; *The Tempest*, 1987; *A Midsummer Night's Dream*, 1994; *Hamlet*, 1995; *King Lear*, 1999; *Pericles*, 2003); Suzuki Tadashi's versions (*The Tale of Lear*, 1984; *The Chronicle of Macbeth*, 1992); Wu HsingKuo's Beijing Opera adaptations (*The Kingdom of Desire* (*Macbeth*), 1986; *Li ErZai Ci* (*King Lear*), 2002); the Kunqu Opera Troupe's *Macbeth* (1987); the *Kathakali King Lear* (1989); the Nomura School's *kyogen* adaptations (*Hora Zamurai*—A *KyogenFalstaff*, 1991; *Kyogen of Errors*, 2001); and the multicultural productions of Ong Keng Sen (*Lear*, 1997; *Desdemona*, 2000; *Search: Hamlet*, 2002)." (See Lan 2005, p. 530; Tuan's retold by chronological rearrangement.).

Ninagawa's *Hamlet*[3] (2015), like his *shingeki*[4]-styled *The Tempest* (1987), incorporated Shakespeare's original script with the pre-modern Japanese Meiji period history, translated from English into Japanese and nourished by intercultural theater. Ninagawa's *Hamlet* is performed in Japanese with Chinese subtitles. Faithfully presenting the whole lines of the play written by Shakespeare, Ninagawa's *Hamlet* opens with the stage set designed by Setsu Asakur to reflect Ninagawa's idea of setting the scene in the Meiji period to pay tribute to the era when *Hamlet* was first staged in Japan. Quoting John Peter's comment (*Sunday Times*, September 8, 1996) on Ninagawa's *Midsummer Night's Dream* (1994), Dennis Kennedy stated that Ninagawa's *Hamlet* is "Shakespeare in Japanese, but it is not really Japanese Shakespeare" (2001, p. 323). In line with this view, I argue that Ninagawa's *Hamlet* played in Taipei in 2015 is a Japanese yet improved Shakespeare, his eighth attempt to stage the genuine Shakespeare in Japanese by intercultural representation.

THE AESTHETICS OF NINAGAWA'S *HAMLET* IN TAIWAN

In the play-within-the-play-within-the-play, Ninagawa represents Shakespeare's the Mouse Trap scene from *Hamlet* with the simulated murder happening twice: in mime and in classical Japanese *kabuki* style. First, the troupe invited by Hamlet uses the mime to stage the murder scene; however, it does not arouse Claudius' attention while he flirts with Gertrude. Second, the audiences, along with the players, watch the Mouse Trap scene play-within-the-play-within-the-play, featuring an interior curtain on the stage in the double theatrical frame, in which the touring troupe, invited by Hamlet, performs by dressing in the spectacular classical

---

[3] This is the eighth time that Ninagawa has directed *Hamlet*.
[4] In the second footnote, *shingeki* is: "a Japanese theatrical movement of encouraging the European modern theatre during the late nineteenth century through the early twentieth century" (the performance program of Ninagawa's*Hamlet*). In Wikipedia, the free Encyclopedia: "*Shingeki*: "(新劇, literally 'new drama') was the leading form of modern theater in Japan in the twentieth century. It was the effort to introduce Western-style realist theatre to Japan, first by presenting the works of Western writers such as Henrik Ibsen, Anton Chekhov, Maxim Gorky, and Eugene O'Neill, but then by producing Japanese works. Performances reflected the styles of Russian proscenium theatre, and some of the elements included realistic/foreign costumes, the use of actresses over *onnagata*, self-contained plots, and, when transferred to film, close-ups." (https://en.wikipedia.org/wiki/Shingeki). Retrieved on June 14, 2015).

Fig. 4.1 The the Mouse Trap scene is staged for the second time in this play-within-the-play-within-the-play in Ninagawa's *Hamlet* (2015) in spectacular beautiful royal court costumes and elegant movement in Japanese *kabuki* style. (Courtesy of Takahiro Watanabe)

Japanese costumes. The movement in the mise-en-scène is slow and elegant, in accordance with the Japanese *kabuki* style (Fig. 4.1).

Both Ninagawa and Ariane Mnouchkine (1939–) use the Japanese *kabuki* style to direct their works: Ninagawa's *Macbeth* (1980) and the second Mouse Trap scene in *Hamlet* (2015); Mnouchkine's *Richard II* (1981). For Leonard C. Pronko, Ninagawa's *Macbeth* and Mnouchkine's *Richard II* are "the most impressive examples of East–West fusion in the professional theatre" (1996, p. 30).

In East–West fusion theater, in my perspective, the Claudius' confession scene encompasses Japanese sadist torture style in which Mikijiro Hiro (playing Claudius/Ghost of Hamlet's Father) takes off his clothes and, wearing merely a white loincloth, pours water from the wooden basket pulled up from the big old Japanese well on the stage. This kind of Japanese sadist self-torture is similar to the ritualistic self-torture of Western European Middle Age religious secret cult monks who used leather belts to whip their bare backs until they bled, as can be seen in the film *The Davinci Code* (2006).

Ninagawa is subtle in his design, dressing the actress playing Ophelia, Hikari Mitsushima, in a white gown—in sharp contrast to the actor playing Hamlet, who wears black—and having her sing Japanese songs to express her insanity through sadness. Those particular scenes not only contain Japanese flavors, but also cover Japanese cultural essences and spirits that touch the audience's heart.

Moreover, the representation in Ninagawa's *Hamlet* of Fortinbras as a man of action and Hamlet as a man of thought explains the contrasting character types in Elizabethan Drama. In Ninagawa's production, Fortinbras appears three times. It is when Hamlet sees Fortinbras marching his army to claim his dead father's lost territory that he transforms from a hesitant man of thought to a revenge-seeking man of action. In my opinion, this theme similarly appears in Shakespeare's other plays, with characters such as Prince Hal and Hotspur in terms of fighting for honor in *Henry IV Part I*. Following advice from King Henry, Prince Hal stops drinking in the pubs and visiting whorehouse with the fat coward Falstaff and begins fighting valiantly against Hotspur, for whom honor is a priority. In his production of *Hamlet*, Ninagawa presents the scene in which Hamlet is transformed by having the actor playing Fortinbras—wearing a blue shirt open with his chest on show—appear with several soldiers waving a big blue army flag in the background. The scene is filled with Japanese Samurai warrior heroic spirit—there is no fear of death in the battlefield.

In his first production of *Hamlet* (1995, Japan) Ninagawa invited actor Hagiwara Ken'ichi, a rock star and a cultural hero, to play the role of Hamlet. By contrast, Tatsuya Fujiwara, a young upcoming actor who had received several drama prizes in Japan, played him in Ninagawa's eighth production of the play. In the first production, Ninagawa also used *Hinamatsuri* (girls' festival) style: "(o)n the night of the festival, Hagiwara Ken'ichi (Hamlet) would appear like a ghost" ("Interview with Ninagawa Yukio." Ryuta. Eds. 2001, p. 209). His eighth production he uses Japanese *shingeki* style in an indelible scene set in the Japanese Meiji period. In this production it appears to me that the team is more important than the individual who plays the role of Hamlet. My idea is supported by Ninagawa's words, "(w)ho plays *Hamlet* may surely affect the overall performance, but ultimately it is always the creativity of the team, including those on and off the stage, that really matters" (2015 Taipei Performance Program, p. 4). After all, theater performance is the creative collaboration of the entire company.

In my view, the young, talented actor Tatsuya Fujiwara's way of playing Hamlet, wearing a black long robe, is more violent (Fig. 4.2) than Sir

Fig. 4.2 Wearing a black long robe, Tatsuya Fujiwara's interpretation of Hamlet, with the hint of Oedipus Complex, is more violent than Sir Laurence Olivier's portrayal of a more classic and melancholy Hamlet (1948 film). (Courtesy of Takahiro Watanabe)

Laurence Olivier's Hamlet (1948 film) who is more classic and melancholic. Fujiwara's portrayal of Hamlet and his Oedipus Complex hints at incest. This is especially apparent in Gertrude's royal chamber scene when he violently pushes Gertrude, wearing only her sleeping gown, down onto his mother's bed and presses his body upon hers, cursing her incest and infidelity toward his deceased father King Hamlet.

In terms of intercultural theater, Dennis Kennedy's concern about "Mnouchkine's Orientalism" or "Ninagawa's Occidentalism" in Shakespearean adaptation might be taken as a measurement and a caution for those intercultural theater artists. "For they should not just create their aesthetic style through cultural pastiche and collage at the price of political valence or social experience" (Kennedy, pp. 296–300). Yet Kennedy has not provided a theory to explain the complicated and dynamic two-way cultural flow in intercultural theater. In my view, in intercultural theater and an East–West fusion performance, directors filter arbitrarily the two cultures through deliberate artistic design, commercial selling, or political purpose in order to market their productions to international audiences. As universal as Shakespeare is, Ninagawa's *Hamlet* (2015) in Taipei seems to have received a more heated audience reception than in Japan and London so far. In general, Taiwan audiences are very hospitable to and receptive of foreign troupes.

AUDIENCE RECEPTION IN TAIWAN

Ninagawa is an icon welcomed and even worshiped by the audiences in Taiwan. Tickets were all sold out long before the flagship production's premiere in Taipei. Ninagawa has directed many Western classics in the past forty-one years, beginning with his first big joint theater piece *Romeo and Juliet* with Producer Mr. Nakane in 1974.[5] He followed that with an overseas tour of *Macbeth* (1980, Japan) in Japanese Samurai style, the first of his Shakespeare productions, at the 1985 Edinburgh Festival. Without doubt, I observe that Ninagawa's production has become a cultural ambassador and Japanese icon for the Taiwanese audiences, to be purchased and consumed as a cultural commodity.

---

[5] In "Interview with Ninagawa Yukio," Ninagawa said: "It was in 1974.... I started thinking about directing Shakespeare after my work with Shimizu had failed." (July 4, 2001. *Performing Shakespeare in Japan*. Eds. Minami Ryuta, Ian Carruthers, John Gillies.).

If everyone (here I mean the English-speaking elite intellectuals) understands Shakespeare, then I argue that the familiar Shakespeare play from England, performed by a Japanese cast, and set in the Meiji period in the Japanese pre-modern colonial era stirs up unfamiliar, foreign, exotic, and even nostalgic feelings for the audiences in Taiwan. Taiwan was colonized by Japan from 1895 to 1945 and even now, postcolonialization, Taiwanese people's ambivalent love–hate feelings toward Japan still linger. Taiwanese audiences' ambivalent nostalgic psychology partially explains why even the older, established Ninagawa has to sell his big name by using his established well-acclaimed status in world theater history. In this *Hamlet* (2015) production, unlike the younger Japanese directors, Ninagawa attempts little new aggressive avant-garde experimental theater, nor does he use breakthrough poetic aesthetics such as Suzuki Tadashi's *Cyrano de Bergerac* (2009, Taipei). Even so, Ninagawa is still very welcomed by the audience members and aficionados in Taiwan.

Through warm receptions in Europe, Ninagawa made his name abroad early in the 1980s. Ninagawa's production aptly entitled *Ninagawa's Macbeth* at the Edinburgh Festival in 1985 was all sellout that received critical acclaim. The English audiences also enjoyed Ninagawa's *The Tempest* (1988), so that it was revived in London in 1992. Nevertheless, as Tetsuo Kishi sharply points out in "Japanese Shakespeare and English Reviewers" in *Shakespeare and the Japanese Stage*, "there is a lot of affinity between traditional Japanese theatre (here, I think Kishi particularly means Noh and Kabuki) and Shakespeare, that is, the kind of affinity which Ninagawa does not seem to have paid much attention to and which most English reviewers do not seem to have been aware of" (p. 119). Both Ninagawa and the English reviewers might neglect or not understand the correct and nuanced details, so the traditional Japanese theater essence elements like *noh* and *kabuki* are not more accurately presented in the historical contextualization. It is just that "the exoticism clouded their eyes" (Kishi 1998, p. 122).

Similar critics' performance reviews can be found in *The Telegraph*, for example, where in her review of a Barbican performance Jane Shilling comments that Ninagawa Company's *Hamlet* included "moments of revelation." Shilling said, "the acclaimed Japanese director's latest production is vivid if arid" (Posted online on May 22, 2015). Even the English reviewers like Shilling observe that, with his *Hamlet* (2015) in Europe, Ninagawa is kind of doing the same dried up, old vivid visual trick of spectacle all the time, yet without creating something new and innovative.

Therefore we should be cautious when interpreting the warm audience reception in Taiwan. First of all, Taiwanese audiences are more willing to watch Ninagawa's *Hamlet* flagship production of the Taiwan International Festival of Arts. It has a huge production budget—it is not a small, low-cost experimental performance produced by a local troupe. Secondly, as Kishi indicates, Taiwan audiences like the foreign and unfamiliar troupes whose exoticism might cloud their judgment. I think Ninagawa has become a cultural commodity for Taiwanese audiences who are willing to purchase the perceived value of a theatrical icon brand.

Thirdly, the audiences in Taiwan might share the same humble attitude as Ninagawa, who indicates that the Japanese feel ashamed when performing Shakespeare's plays, for it represents a high-brow culture and Western imperialism and colonialism. So, in the similar Far Eastern or in the same Asian shoes, the audience members in Taiwan admire Ninagawa, because he, as an Asian, has won recognition from English and European audiences and critics by representing Shakespeare's plays in his Japanese traditional theater style.

CONCLUSION

I use Indian theater scholar Rustom Bharucha's criticism on Peter Brook's *The Mahabaharata* as being the Western cultural hegemony to argue that Taiwanese audiences may feel the same way about Ninagawa's *Hamlet* in terms of Asian authenticity and identity. In Bharucha's view, Brook appropriates this work to cater for the Western audiences without a genuine understanding of the underlying meaning of this Indian epic. Taiwanese audiences, like Japanese audiences, recognize and value their masterpieces, theatrical heritage, and Asian identities. As such, Asian audiences may respond to Ninagawa's works on Shakespeare in a different way. Asians do not perform Shakespeare's Western classics just as a universal value, but also with authoritative Asian artistic direction; to create intercultural performativity.

No doubt, Ninagawa's productions are full of visual spectacle. However, this spectacle may lead to a view like that of Yeeyon Im, who says in her "The Pitfalls of Intercultural Discourse: The Case of Yukio Ninagawa":

> The problem of Ninagawa's Shakespeare productions, scholars have argued, is his unscrupulous Orientalism that caters for the Western audiences, an easy pitfall to which the so-called intercultural theatre can become prey. (2004, p. 7)

This suggests that an audience like Yeeyon Im would praise Ninagawa's Shakespeare productions more if he added more authentic Eastern cultural elements and theatrical styles in his works. By incorporating such elements and styles, Ninagawa may simultaneously preserve the intercultural theater characteristics and please the Western and Asian audiences with his visual spectacles. For instance, Ninagawa's artistic design teamwork includes the Japanese architecture in the stage design, set design, and costume design. Ninagawa not only presents the visual effects imbued with Japanese style, but also offers the aural by using the Japanese translation of Shakespeare's seventeenth century archaic English for the audience. Actually, for the audience members who do not understand Japanese, the dialogues, monologues, and conversations spoken and performed by the actors and actresses are just Japanese language sounds. The audience members may experience German playwright Bertolt Brecht's theory of "Alienation Effect," and keep an aesthetic distance while watching Ninagawa's Shakespeare productions in Japanese. The stories in Shakespeare's plays, such as *Hamlet*, are so well known that they are both a global cultural heritage and human legacy. The audiences can also understand the plot courtesy of the English subtitles, but, moreover, they feel the emotions created by the cast's physical performances, gestures, facial expressions, and tone differences.

To demonstrate the audience reception in Taiwan, I quote the comment (in Chinese) of an audience member under the penname "milanhime" in a blog: "the set designed by Setsu Asakura and Tsukasa Nakagoshi is good looking, very attractive" (my English translation). Compared to other Shakespeare performances staged in Taiwan by overseas troupes, such as Shakespeare in Russian and Shakespeare in Dutch, it is much easier for Taiwanese audiences to comprehend Ninagawa's *Hamlet* (2015, Taipei) by understanding the authentic English lines of Shakespeare's play and through the previous experience of watching *Shamlet* (a comedy in Chinese radically adapted from and inspired by Shakespeare's *Hamlet*), created by Taiwanese artistic director and actor Lee, Kuo-Hsiu (1955–2013). Both Shakespeare's play *Hamlet* in English and Lee's production *Shamlet* in Chinese help the local Taiwanese audiences to understand Ninagawa's *Hamlet* in Japanese, without feeling too tired to watch the performance, even after work.[6]

---

[6] This audience reception is collected from the blog where the audience member expressed that he didn't feel tired after work when he watched Ninagawa's production.

This chapter argues that both authentic Japanese cultural roots and Western–Asian intercultural impact are apparent in Ninagawa's *Hamlet*. "Who are you?" asked Ninagawa, while he embraced the contemporary Japan in performing *Hamlet*. I propose that the "filter theory" from Patrice Pavis' book *Intercultural Performance Reader*, is apparent in the case of Ninagawa's *Hamlet*. Ninagawa uses his source culture alongside the Western culture of Shakespeare's English play. Attention to the detail of these cultures can be observed, for example, in the last fight scene between Hamlet and Laertes, who really is trained to use rapiers to fight the Western thin and long fencing swords (which appeared in the fifteenth century in Europe). Moreover, cultural interaction and the combined flow of two cultures are achieved through Ninagawa's addition of the target culture through traditional Japanese theater style. For instance, Ninagawa shows the character Fortinbras as a man of action, with Japanese Samurai warrior spirit.

Ninagawa's *Hamlet* (2015) in Taiwan is imbued with film techniques employed in today's media age. For example, modern media technique is employed after the troupe's simulation of the old King Hamlet's murder in the second Mouse Trap scene—for Hamlet to test if his uncle, new King Claudius, really has murdered his father. Claudius suddenly leaves with shock, shame, guilt, and anger. The actors perform Shakespeare's original English lines:

Ophelia: The king rises.
Hamlet: What, frighted with false fire?
Queen: How fares my lord?
Polonius: Give o'er the play.
King: Give me some light. Away!
Polonius: Lights, lights, lights!
           Exeunt all but Hamlet and Horatio.
(III. ii. 265–271)

I think this part reflects (or resonates with) German professor and theater scholar Erika Fischer-Lichte's theory of "Retheatricalization" of the play. Her "Retheatricalization as productive reception of Far Eastern Theatre" is particularly suitable for staging Far Eastern intercultural performances of Shakespeare in Asian languages. To emphasize visual cultures and spectacles, Ninagawa directed glaring white lights onto certain characters to exaggerate the stage effect. He also employed the cinematic techniques of slow motion, freezing movements, and sharp lights to show the characters and players' grotesque acts of climbing on the floor, falling down on the floor, and upside down movement; all of which, I think, are symbolic of corrupt politics. Both the Elizabethan classical drama of Shakespeare and the Japanese traditional theater styles like *kabuki* are affinities. Ninagawa's use of spectacles, including the exotic and oriental elements, appeals to Taiwan audiences' nostalgic feelings toward Japan. The above accounts explain why Shakespeare in Asia is so popular and why Ninagawa's *Hamlet* is well acclaimed by Taiwanese audiences. Ninagawa's *Hamlet* (2015) in Taiwan is a representative East–West fusion and intercultural performance. Ninagawa's accomplishments in theater are remembered even if he has passed away.

Bibliography

Brokering, Jon M. "Ninagawa Yukio's Intercultural *Hamlet*: Parsing Japanese Iconography." *Asian Theatre Journal*, 2007, Vol. 24 (2), pp. 370–397.

Ellis, Samantha. G2: Arts: 'Some people can't let it go': As Yukio Ninagawa's sixth production of *Hamlet* opens, Samantha Ellis asks directors why they return to the play. (Guardian Features Pages). Yukio Ninagawa, Richard Eyre, Trevor Nunn And Jonathan Kent. *The Guardian* , Sept 29, 2004, p.11.

Hickling, Alfred. "Saturday review: Arts: Doctor Noh: Japan's traditional theatre is so dull it sends entire audiences to sleep. If anyone can spice things up, it's Yukio Ninagawa." Alfred Hickling meets the great ashtray-flinging director. (Guardian Saturday Pages). *The Guardian* , May 19, 2001, p.5.

Im, Yeeyon. "The pitfalls of intercultural discourse: the case of Yukio Ninagawa." (Critical Essay). *Shakespeare Bulletin*. Winter, 2004, Vol. 22 (4), 2004, pp. 7–24.

Kennedy, Dennis. *Looking at Shakespeare: A Visual History of Twentieth-Century Performance*. 2nd Edition. UK: Cambridge University Press, 2001, pp. 296–300.

Kishi, Tetsuo (1998). "Japanese Shakespeare and English Reviewers." In Takashi Sasayama, J. R. Mulryne, and Margaret Shewring. Eds. *Shakespeare and the Japanese Stage*. Cambridge: Cambridge UP. pp. 110–123.

Lichte, Fischer Erika. *The Show and the Gaze of Theatre: A European Perspective*. Iowa: University of Iowa Press, 1997.

Lan, Yong Li. (2005). "Shakespeare and the Fiction of the Intercultural." In Barbara Hodgdon and W. B. Worthen. Eds. *A Companion to Shakespeare and Performance*. Oxford: Blackwell, pp. 527–549.

Pavis, Patrice. *The Intercultural Performance Reader*. London and Routledge, 1996.

Pronko, Leonard C. (1996). "Approaching Shakespeare through Kabuki." In Minoru Fujita and Leonard Pronko, eds. Shakespeare: East and West. Surrey: Japan Lib. pp. 23–40.

Ryuta, Minami, Carruthers, Ian & Gillies, John. Eds. (2001). "Interview with Ninagawa Yukio." *Performing Shakespeare in Japan*. Cambridge: Cambridge UP, pp. 208–219.
Shakespeare, William. "The Tragedy of Hamlet, Prince of Denmark." *The Riverside Shakespeare*. Boston: Houghton Mifflin Company, 1974, pp. 1135–1197.
Shilling, Jane. "Ninagawa Company's *Hamlet*: Barbican, review: moments of revelation." *The Telegraphy*. Posted on May 22, 2015. http://www.telegraph.co.uk/culture/theatre/theatre-reviews/11619191/Ninagawa-Companys-Hamlet-Barbican-review-moments-of-revelation.html. Retrieved on June 12, 2015.
Yo, Zushi. "Forks in the road come suddenly. I take the dangerous route": Yukio Ninagawa, theatre director. (The NS Interview) (Interview) *New Statesman*. (1996), June 18, 2012, Vol. 141 (5110), p. 38(2).

Websites

Yukio Ninagawa at the Internet Movie Database.
NINAGAWA STUDIO WEBSITE.
Audience reception in Taiwan. Milanhime. http://milanhime.pixnet.net/blog/post/30785914-2015%E8%A7%80%E5%8A%87--%E8%9C%B7%E5%B7%9D%E5%B9%B8%E9%9B%84%E3%80%8A%E5%93%88%E5%A7%86%E9%9B%B7%E7%89%B9%E3%80%8B-hamlet-by-yukio-n. Posted on March 26, 2015. Retrieved on June 16, 2015.

CHAPTER 5

Theater Represents Literature: Love and Labor in *To Send Away Under Escort*

Abstract This chapter explores love and labor in the performance of *To Send Away Under Escort* (《押解》) (October 31 2015, Jhubei City Performance Hall) staged by Greenray Theatre Company. Playwright Wu, Nien-Chen collaborates with comedic director Li, Ming-Tse to adapt the novel written by Mr. Tuan, Tsai-Hua. Intertextuality contains Peking opera singing *Sue-San Being Sent Under Escort*. In the performance, the character Policeman Huang suggests that the protagonist Ho take care of his fruit garden, a metaphor for Ho's mistresses. Although the leads characters are male, the female characters play important roles, visible or invisible, in propelling the plot. The themes of this play are compassion, empathy, law, and love. Nostalgia, local politics, and pre-martial law relate to the universal theme of love.

Keywords Literature • Performance • Language • Greenray Theatre Company • Politics

INTRODUCTION

Theater represents literature; that is, theatrical arts can bring the words of literature to life. Theater can also visualize the imagination. As William Shakespeare in the play *Love's Labour's Lost* describes, love takes effort and labor is required to win the beauty's heart. Literature, by labor of adaptation from script to performance, works as cultural capital to revitalize Asian performance. This chapter explores the theme of love and labor in the Greenray Theatre Company's October 31, 2015 performance of *To Send Away under Escort* at Jhubei City Performance Hall in Taiwan.

Greenray Theatre Company, established in 1993, has staged five types of production—(1) (original) Chinese musicals, (2) citizen drama, (3) world theater, (4) Taiwan literature theater, and (5) metropolitan living theater. In the genre of Taiwan literature theater, the series of works called "Human Condition" have been produced by Greenray Theatre Company since the premiere of the first in the series *Tomb-Sweeping Season* (《清明時節》) (October 2010, Taipei City Hall): the second in the series was *The Single Temperature* (《單身溫度》) (premiered March 2013, National Theater in Taipei). When deciding what they would do for the third in the series, artistic supervisor and film director Ke, Yi-Cheng proposed that artistic supervisor and playwright Wu, Nien-Chen had adapted Mr. Tuan Tsai-Hua's short novel *To Send Away Under Escort* (《押解》) thirty years ago and had already outlined the scenes in anticipation of shooting the movie. However, the movie was never made, because the Railroad Bureau would not lend them a train—the setting for most of the story. Their reason for refusal was that people such as the character Pickpocket were not allowed on trains in the strict, conservative pre-martial law era of the time. After thirty years, in the twenty-first century, Ke encouraged Wu to adapt Tuan's novel into a stage performance script. They invited theater comedic director Li, Ming-Tse to join them to do a script adaptation. TV actor Tang Tsung-Sheng and actress Ray Fan, both of whom excel in performing comedy, were also recruited. The aim was to represent Taiwan literature through theatrical art.

Playwright Tuan's Writing Style

The stage performance *To Send Away Under Escort* emphasizes love and labor. Artistic supervisor and playwright Wu collaborated with director Li to adapt the novel of the same title written by Mr. Tuan, Tsai-Hua (1933–2015).

Writer Tuan is good at employing motion picture description to create in his novels the cinematic effect of montage. The background for most of his stories are in his hometown, the army, or other real-life situations. Tuan's works, full of human spirit, deeply explore human nature, expounding and propagating justice.

In the 1950s in Taiwan, due to politics with China and the economic situation, the people's lives were not rich. Wu thinks that "Writer Tuan was different from the Taiwanese writers in the 1950s, because at that time the writers' styles are usually sad and meditative. In a comparison, Writer Tuan's personality is quiet. However, his words make him like a Porker-faced comedian for he often wrote some literature of humor. All of the small potatoes' images are very vivid. All of the scenes let you feel you look at the pictures. Reading his articles is like seeing a movie. The work *Send Away Under Escort* is just like that kind of a humorous short novel." (Program 2015, p. 4) Even in the tough times, Writer Tuan wrote the novels with humor. Therefore in the story we have empathy with the Pickpocket character Ho (played by Tang Tsung-Sheng). We understand why Ho tries to escape under escort by the good but naïve rookie policeman Hwang (played by Huang Di-Yang), because he just wants to see his old sick grandma before she dies, and then he will come back to the prison. Actor Tang performs the magic tricks of escaping from the handcuffs and the rope on stage (Fig. 5.1).

Fig. 5.1 Actor Tang Tsung-Sheng (playing the role of Pickpocket Ho) performs the magic tricks of escaping from the handcuffs and the rope on stage (left). The naïve Hwang (the role is played by Huang Di-Yang) (right). (Courtesy of Greenray Theatre Company)

Feminism

Despite the leads being two male characters, the women characters—including Grandma, Ho's three mistresses, and Yo Yu-Mei (Rookie Policeman Hwang's middle-school classmate)—play important roles in the plot. Ho's three mistresses do not have actual names, just the nicknames Orange, Litchi, and Peach. Only the former two women Orange (played by actress Dai Hsiu-Yin) and Litchi (played by actress Chiang Yo-Lien) appear visibly on stage, Peach is invisible and only mentioned by the male characters. As Professor Sue-Ellen Case in *Feminism and Theatre* points out:

> As a result of the suppression of real women, the culture invented its own ... and it was this fictional "Woman" who appeared on stage, in the myths and in the plastic arts, representing the patriarchal values attached to the gender while suppressing the experiences, stories, feelings and the fantasies of the actual women. (See Teresa de Lauretis for a development of this concept. (What) distinguishes this "Woman" as a male-produced fiction from historical women. (1998, p. 7)

Distinguished Professor Case, in this influential book, indicates that the notion of woman is different from the real and historical women, but invented as a culturally constructed product. I think that this performance goes further than what Lizbeth Goodman elucidates as Laura Mulvey's notion of "woman as image and man as the bearer of the look" (p. 272), because this performance strengthens some female roles. For example, the actresses act the female roles of Grandma in the caring image of Saint Mary, mother of God. Yo is seen as the boy's fantasy angel.

Physical performance also counts. According to Jeanie Forte in "Focus on the Body: Pain, Praxis, and Pleasure in Feminist Performance," "For feminists postmodernist theory enables an understanding of gender within culture and in relation to the supposed referentiality of the female body and shifts focus on the body in representational systems." (p. 248). Woman no longer exists just in images or representation, but in physical embodiment to be seen and heard through her actual experience perspective.

We may admit to agreeing with Forte that "(i)t has also become next to impossible, however, to discuss the female body without having to discursively 'skirt' around it, as it were, and field charges of essentialism." (p. 248). To "skirt" around the obstacles of essentialism, not limited to the good Grandma, angelic middle-school sweet heart, and the men's spiritual and physical mistresses, theater performances should create more unconventional female roles and represent the female body in other innovative ways.

We can't theorize the body, because "the body has no apparatus." However, as Jane Gallop notes, talking about "the body raises the specter of referentiality, the threat of slipping into a thematics of the body, as if there were a 'body itself,' unmediated by textuality" (p. 248). Through textual reference, in this performance, we hear the ancient story of the piteous woman *Sue-San Being Sent Under Escort*. Paradoxically, Sue-San's sad story is physically acted out by the male lead actor, Tang. Referentiality, as is the tradition of Chinese Beijing opera, male actors, such as the famous actor Mei, Lan-fang, played the female roles. It proves that women's bodies can be culturally constructed by men's fictional imagination.

The fruit names given to the mistresses somehow symbolize the female body, with sexual associations. I would like to suggest that complex female characters can be created by the stimulus of theoretical tenets, such as Jill Dolan's concept of ideology and sexuality, and Sue Ellen Case's analysis of gender in performance.

NOSTALGIA AND LOCAL APPEAL TO UNIVERSAL AND GLOBAL

As already mentioned, the themes of this play are compassion, empathy, law, and love. Use of nostalgia and local politics (pre-martial law) appeal to the universal love. Journalist Wang Wan-Chun reports that director Li expressed, in the former performances staged in Taipei and Taichung in 2015, that they add current events, such as Kuomintang (KMT) (Chinese Nationalist Party)'s sudden replacement of the female presidential candidate Hung Hsiu-Chu by the male candidate Chu Li-Lun, and Democratic Progressive Party (DDP)'s president candidate Tsai Yin-Wen's run in the campaigns to compete with KMT. Taiwan's hot local political presidential campaign attracted global attention, including CNN in the US and China. Eventually, Tsai got more votes to become the first female president in Taiwan in 2016.

The male lead actor Tang expresses his opinion of playing the role, his experiences in taking the train, and his feelings about this performance. Tang thinks that this play is about love, friendship, and family emotions. Tang acts, sings, and does a little dance in this production. He plays the role of Ho, who tries hard to escape from prison in order to see his old sick grandma before she dies. In the scene where Ho says good-bye to his grandma (Fig. 5.2), the actor Tang feels like being separated in life and death is to part forever. Tang says that this is a part he plays from his real-life experience.

Fig. 5.2 Actor Tang (playing the role of pickpocket Ho), kneeling down to express his filial piety, finally meets his adopted grandmother who is old, sick, and near dying. In the center right, Ray Fan plays the role of the old Grandma. To the left, the good, naïve rookie policeman (played by Huang Di-Yang) is moved to agree to accompany Ho to pay the visit and then escort him back to the prison. On the right, Orange (played by actress Dai Hsui-Yin), who is in love with Ho, waits for him, taking care of his grandma for many years. (Courtesy of Greenray Theatre Company)

From Literature to Performance

Tuan's short novel in today's perspective might seem nostalgic, full of the milieu of remembering the past years. Though the people's lives in Taiwan in the 1950s were poor, their hearts were very pure and more innocent. Comparatively, although we enjoy better material lives in the economic situation in the twenty-first century, some people's hearts get soiled with jealousy and pettiness. A lot of ugly politics happen in society, in the two parties' political campaigns, for example, and in academia as well. We should still have compassion and empathy without bullying oppression and fake justice.

Justice and law are not as simple as they appear on the surface. This is demonstrated in this production by the young policeman who finally comes to understand how to balance severe law and poetic justice. He, without really releasing the prisoner, finds a balance by taking Ho, under his escort, back to Ho's hometown on a remote mountain to see his old sick grandma and fulfill his wish.

During the process, the young policeman also learns how to pursue the girl he likes from his childhood, the way the world works, and the difference between the ideal and the reality. At the end of the performance, he sends Ho back to the prison, they become friends, and everything ends happily. This is a nice touching comedy, without going too extremes to be dogmatic, and without melodrama. This performance is full of lessons taught through laughter and tears.

To add theatricality and intertextuality, the modern drama *Huaju* stage performance also contains the Peking opera singing *Sue-San Being Sent under Escort* scene. In the famous Peking opera repertory, the story is that in ancient China the innocent poor woman Sue-San was wronged when sent to the prison. On the way, while under escort, Sue-San sings about her sorrow and laments over the injustice. This modern drama stage performance uses the ancient metaphor of echoing Sue-San's ancient story and narrates anecdotes of the past in alluding to the present. Tang performs Ho's story on stage through Peking opera stylization while dressed in contemporary costume in this scene. It is interesting to combine Peking opera with stage drama performance to demonstrate the high levels of performing skill.

The cast play well in this moving, emotion-filled performance. Except for the two male leads, almost every other performer plays more than one role. The action takes place mostly on the train. Tang, the male lead, is good at playing the difficult role of Ho Chin-Fa. Ho's job is a pickpocket, he is not a decent man with the regular legal vocation. However, Tang skillfully makes the audience empathize with this character. The audience believe that Ho is actually righteous, with a good heart, just forced to steal to make a living to support his old grandma who adopted him when he was a little orphan. Tuan, Wu, Li, and Tang make this "neither black nor white" character Ho into a human being, gaining the audiences' empathy.

The cast includes Ray Fan (Best Supporting Actress of the Golden Bell Award in 1997), who plays the two roles of the old Grandma and the Missionary. Fan (1972–) is made-up and dressed to look like an old grandma and she plays the role of an elderly dementia sufferer well. She makes the audience sob in the scene in which, even though she has memory loss, her concern is for her adopted grandson Ho.

The two actors Chu Yu-Hung and Lai, Chen-Tse, each of whom plays three roles (including Ho's gangster friends—A-Chiang and Marshal), contribute to advancing the comedy. Chu play A-Chiang, Chicken Rice, and Iron Hammer; Lai plays Marshal, Walking Catfish, and Long-legged. These character pairs come together in the subsequent scenes to help the male lead Ho in the process of trying to escape. A-Chiang (who's strong and tall) cooperates with Marshal (who's nervous, incapable, yet faithful) to make a living by lying and confidence tricks. Moreover, Chu plays the role of Iron Hammer (who is an autistic child with the talent to cite Chinese poetry to express his ideas) marvelously. Chu even changes his voice, pronunciation, and the way he speaks to play this autistic child role. On stage after the performance, Chu said that he has observed autistic children in the hospital so that he could understand how they feel and behave in order to portray this role well. Furthermore, the other actors and actresses also play the supporting roles wonderfully.

Theater critic and theater director Fu Yu-Hui highly praises this performance. According to Fu:

> I finally have the chance to see Actor Tang, Tsung-Sheng (who used to be regard as a comedian and a TV show host) deeply interpret a concrete character … Many sharp theatrical body actions and clear efficient neat movements in several scenes create the modern comic funny atmosphere which can be compared to European and Broadway productions, such as the Broadway Comedy: *Boeing Boeing*. The design and creative ideas in modern theater make this production exceed the other series works of "Human Condition." Although there are not so many places for stage design, music design, and projection design to display, they use their concepts and creative ideas to embellish this performance. In the first Act before the intermission, dozens of changing perspectives from the train in those scenes reveal the clever, wonderful imagination that adds the crucial touch.[1]

In my view, the actors Tang, Chu, and Lai can do *lazzi*, an improvised comic dialogue or action commonly used in the Commedia dell'arte. They utilize their experiences as comedian, TV show host, and stage performers well in this live performance.

Chang Chen-Chou in *PAR: Performing Arts Review* expresses his ideas that *To Send Away Under Escort—The Young Rookie Policeman and the Old Pickpocket* continues the strong ancient touching qualities of human kindness and hospitality of Taiwan which the first in the series *Tomb-Sweeping*

---

[1] This is my translation from Fu's comments in Chinese into English.

Season and the second *The Single Temperature* contain. These elements touch a common nerve. The difference is that under Tuan Tsai-Hua's pen, *To Send Away Under Escort* is interesting and full of fun.[2]

Wu, Nien-Chen thinks that "The old Taiwanese writers' many good works are gradually to be forgotten. I hope that I can represent their works in stage performances. By so doing, we can not only let more young people know the old writers of Taiwan, but also give them tributes" (Program 4). And that is also one of my motivations, to find suitable stage performance adapted from literature, so we can preserve the value of literature in this e-era.

Conclusion

It needs love and labor to create theater.[3] It takes a lot of effort for the character Ho to escape to see his old sick grandma before she dies. Theater can make the literary words vivid and impressive. Even when writers pass away, their good literature works can be remembered through theater production. Writing and theater both need persistence. No matter whether the train is slow or fast, this performance appeals due to the themes of love, compassion, caring, bonds, empathy, sympathy, family and friendship, human emotions and feelings, which are everlasting. Those abstract feelings can be visualized in theater performance. And literature can be represented by theater.

Literature can be transformed from different genres—from novel to script, and then into performance—with the hard work of adaptation and mixing languages (Mandarin and Taiwanese dialect) as a cultural capital in revitalizing Asian performance. Theater represents literature. Love and labor can be seen in the performance *To Send Away Under Escort*. It is a good and effective way to pay tribute to the old Taiwanese writers by using stage performances to represent the excellent literature works.

Bibliography

Case, Sue-Ellen. 1998. *Feminism and Theatre*. New York: Routledge.
Chang, Chen-Chou. 2015. *PAR: Performing Arts Review*. (《表演藝術雜誌》). https://www.artsticket.com.tw/CKSCC2005/Product/Product00/ProductsDetailsPage.aspx?ProductID=oK4bYlG1Gfw2l5nOQcInDQ. Retrieved on June 27, 2016.

[2] This is my translation from Chang's comments in Chinese into English.
[3] Echo to the theme of the international theater conference ATHE in 2016 on "Labor."

Dolan, Jill. 1989. "In Defense of the Discourse: Materialist Feminism, Postmodernism, Poststructuralism and Theory." *The Drama Review* 33: 69.

———. "Ideology in Performance: Looking through the Male Gaze." *The Feminist Spectator as Critic*. Ann Arbor: UMI Research Press, 1988.

Forte, Jeanie. "Focus on the Body: Pain, Praxis, and Pleasure in Feminist Performance." *Critical Theory and Performance*. Ed. Janelle G. Reinelt and Joseph R. Roach. Ann Arbor: The University of Michigan Press, 1992, pp. 248–262.

Goodman, Lizbeth, and Gay, de Jane. *The Routledge Reader in Politics and Performance*. London: Routledge, 2000.

Program. 2015. *To Send Away Under Escort*(押解). Taipei: Greenray Theatre Company.

Fu, Yu-Hui. 2015. Performance Review. https://www.artsticket.com.tw/CKSCC2005/Product/Product00/ProductsDetailsPage.aspx?ProductID=oK4bYlG1Gfw2l5nOQcInDQ. Retrieved on June 27, 2016.

Tuan, Tsai-Hua. 2006. *Selection of Tuan, Tsai-Hua's Novels*. (《段彩華小說選集》). Taipei: The Commercial Press, Ltd.

Yen, Hung-Ya. 2016. *New Millennium Taiwan Theater*. Taipei: Wunan.

Liu, Wan-Chun. 2015. "Greenray Theatre Company's *To Send Away Under Escort* Tour Performance." *Liberty Times*. Posted on Nov. 5. http://www.greenray.org.tw/yajie/news.html. Retrieved on June 27, 2016.

PART II

From Local to Global: Hakka, Dance, Chinese Musical, and Film

CHAPTER 6

Change of Hakka Opera: Ethnicity and Creation in Hakka Musical and Hakka TV Drama

Abstract This chapter explores *My Daughter's Wedding* (the first Hakka musical, an adaptation from Shakespeare's *The Taming of the Shrew*) and *The Ninth Sister of Yang* (an original Hakka Drama, performed by Sin-Yong-Guang Troupe, played on Hakka TV) in Taipei. Hakka opera develops to become Hakka musical and Hakka TV drama to reflect the translocal culture promulgated by government's local cultural policy via media. I focus on the issue of marriage anxiety in the roles of Liu, Li-Chun (Katherina in Shakespeare's play, played by Hsu, Yan-Ling) and Chung, Yo-Chia (Petruchio in Shakespeare's play, played by Huang, Shi-Wei) in *My Daughter's Wedding* and adaptation in *The Ninth Sister of Yang* to argue how Hakka Opera is shifting from tradition to new processes of creation.

Keywords Hakka opera • Hakka musical • *My Daughter's Wedding* • *The Ninth Sister of Yang* • Tradition and creation

BACKGROUND OF HAKKA CULTURE, COMMUNITY, AND PERFORMANCE FORMS

The conflict and settlement of early translocal immigration can be shown through Hakka, a minority ethnicity in Taiwan as a whole. Hakka people as one ethnicity branch immigrated from Fujian and Guandong provinces in south China, to Taiwan, Indonesia, Malaysia, Singapore, and so on in Asia. Hakka has also immigrated to about a Hundred countries around the world, including America.[1] Hakka culture is noteworthy for Hakka people's diligence, frugality, loyalty, and righteousness. The community is united together.[2] The history of Hakka opera originates in the southern part of Jiangxi Province in Mainland China and has been promoted in Taiwan since the end of Qing Dynasty (1875–1911). With the changing times, in order to cater for audiences' tastes in modern proscenium theater, pop entertainment like TV, and film, Hakka three-role tea-picking drama in Taiwan has gradually developed into Hakka rectified drama and Hakka opera. To keep up with audience preference, Hakka opera is now performed in the indoor theaters, there are Hakka musicals, and Hakka drama on TV.

Hakka drama performances are for celebration, worship, and enjoyment in agricultural society. "Tea-picking" serves as the entertainment in daily lives. The performance style is one actor plus one actress or one actor plus two actresses. The main plot is based on Zhang's story of picking tea. The theater of *tea-picking* is influenced by Peking opera, Shu-ping opera, and Luantan opera, performing through singing, reciting, acting, and fighting. Flat tune (平板) is the main melody. It is often a narrative with a few conflicts and a happy ending. Nowadays, traditional performance has been losing its audience. From the perspective of cultural industries, traditional art is viewed as the entertainment of the minority and financial aid comes only from the government. In addition, there are limitations in the plot, music, and language. Therefore it is difficult for Hakka opera to break through this bottleneck. The original function of Hakka opera is religion and entertainment. It offered the village people low-cost entertainment by inviting the Hakka drama troupes to perform for the Buddha and Dao deities on the outdoor stage in front of the temples to appreciate the gods and pray for good harvests. However, the community has changed because the Hakka language-speaking population in Taiwan are a minority nowadays among the Mandarin language-speaking Han ethnicity. Losing the audiences, the decay of Hakka opera is in crisis, especially when facing the attraction of films and computer games in the e-era in the twenty-first century.

---

[1] Source from Hakka Culture Park in Maoli, Taiwan.
[2] Hakka community used to live in big round buildings in the nineteenth century in China, to be united together, to resist the enemy, and to help each other as one big family.

Hakka Drama

The historical development of Hakka drama in Taiwan has progressively evolved from the traditional Hakka three-role tea drama to Hakka rectified drama and Hakka opera, until eventually developing into Hakka musical and Hakka opera on TV. This transformation reflects how, under the influence of Westernization and globalization, the performing arts has sought out originality in the process of modernization, to endow performances with new cultural translocal creativity. *My Daughter's Wedding* (2007), the first Hakka musical, adapted from Shakespeare's *The Taming of the Shrew*, was staged at the National Theater in Taiwan. It subsequently gave birth to a new style of Hakka musicals. This first Hakka musical added modernity and presented Hakka elements with American Broadway musical style, eliminating the secondary story-within-the-story and the overly misogynist tones originally in Shakespeare's play. This first Hakka musical successfully transformed the traditional Hakka drama enough to attract large audiences, breaking down the barrier of Hakka ethnicity and gaining audiences nation-wide of non-Hakka ethnicity as well as foreigners.

Translocally, the hardship of immigrating from China to Taiwan is portrayed in the preface of *The Dance of Carrying Pole* and *The Dance of Tea-picking and Sowing*. In the beginning of the performance there are a group of male dancers in the upper-left of the stage exposing their upper bodies while holding a carrying pole on their shoulders and simulating the action of working hard. On the bottom-left of the stage, two dancers have a fight. Suddenly, the stage becomes the fighting scene and, with the carrying poles as weapons, a ferocious battle begins. The red carpet, pulled by the female dancers, symbolizes the blood and the murdered residents who were trying to protect their home. Then a group of tea-picking girls, bent over and in a neat row, pick the tea in a graceful dance style.

Performativity can broaden the translocal boundary between reality and performance, as Judith Butler proclaims, by repeated performative acts practiced in daily lives. Theater studies has already begun to advance, Andrew Parker and Eve Kosofsky Sedgwick write:

> beyond the classical ontology of the black box model to embrace a myriad of performance practices, ranging from stage to festival and everything in between: film, photography, television, computer simulation, music, "performance art," political demonstrations, health care, cooking, fashion, shamanistic ritual (p. 167)

With translocal performativity, as with the concept of "performativity" in performance studies, theater studies has tried to cross the boundaries of the indoor proscenium stage, and expand to include performing arts, giving a speech, walking, and gesturing in everyday lives.

Performing the everyday lives actions for making a living, a group of male dancers, with blankets in their left hands while sowing with their right hands, immediately appear in the scene. *The Dance of Tea-picking and Sowing* is expressed by dance movements to symbolize the settlement of early Hakka immigration visualized through martial arts and dance choreography.

CHALLENGES IN INNOVATIONS AND ATTRACTING NEW AUDIENCES

Faced with threats of decadence and the possibility of losing their audience—and spurned by modernization and Westernization taking place—the Council for Hakka Affairs in Taiwan took on the similarly impossible task of trying to revive Hakka drama. Li, Yong-Der, Chairman of the Council for Hakka Affairs, believes that incorporating Hakka cultural elements into the modern musical can create a new form of Hakka musical culture. *My Daughter's Wedding*, sponsored by the Council for Hakka Affairs under cultural policy, directed by Chiang, Wei-Kuo from Hong Kong, was the first big production and big budget Hakka musical. *My Daughter's Wedding* (October 2007) demonstrates Asian performance's advance in translocal cultural mobilities to make good use of Western classics, such as Shakespeare's plays.

My Daughter's Wedding is performed in the style of a Broadway musical, reinterpreting Hakka youth's opinion of love and popularizing Hakka opera culture. This script was written by a team of several drama scholars including Lin, Chien-Hua, Wang, Yu-Hui, and Huang Yu-Shan. The performance won acclaim from both critics and audiences.

Why choose Shakespeare's play? Because from Broadway to London's West End, all producers believe that a good story is the backbone to a successful musical. Japanese Shiki Theater Company's founder and well known director Keita Asari once said that "The importance of a musical is the script, which occupying 80%, the music 15%, and everything else 5%." This is the reason the creators of this first Hakka musical chose to use Shakespeare's *The Taming of the Shrew*, to make sure of successful box office sales. Shakespeare's works have continued to be adapted all over the world for performances; whether on stage, on the silver screen, in comics, or through animation. In Taiwan, Shakespeare's plays appear most often in literary works or in the theater, and local theater troupes continue to perform the translated adaptations with undying enthusiasm and devotion.

Due to its literary structure, controversial subject matter, and unique characters, *The Taming of the Shrew* has always been a favorite and has been rewritten into countless adaptations. Hsieh, Jun-Bai, in "The Strategy for Taming *The Taming of the Shrew*: A Literary and Performance Analysis," analyzes the different ways in which playwrights, stage directors, main actors, and movie directors have dealt with the difficult theme of male chauvinism, and sorted out six strategies. Combining historical data from countries such as England and America and then conducting analysis on the presentation of *The Taming of the Shrew* on stage, the six strategies are analyzed as "thorough farce-fiction," "obvious stylization," "emphasized historicism," "raised meta-theater consciousness, "exaggerated emotions," and "emphasized vulgarity." These strategies are different ways to distance/alienate the savagery of the original script. They do not answer the question brought up by Shakespeare about "a story of taming," and even avoid the original crisis in the story.

Why does "a story of taming" make one, so to speak, and then stop? George Bernard Shaw thinks it is about egoism and the sense of masculine superiority. Denton J. Snider thinks the wife is the slave of her husband. E. K. Chambers has sympathy with Katherina for "the shrew is locked by the chain of masculine autarchy." George R. Hibbard points out that the females are regarded as private property. They are not able to enjoy being courted because they are shamed and suppressed. Irving Ribner thinks the taming school glosses over attempts to make the shrew believe the false impression and finally be degraded to animal level. Robert Ornstein believes that "two people are with one heart" is actually "the same as his heart." His view of marriage does not allow the possibility of respect for one another. (Chu 2006, pp. 366–372, my translation).

AMERICAN MUSICAL THEATER

The musical originated from the English light opera, which evolved into the musical comedy or musical theater in Colonial America. According to Wang, Jun-Ting, the musical can be defined as "having music, being musical, and accompanied by music" (Wang 2006). The Broadway musical began as an entertainment industry that had sprung up alongside one of New York's streets, but nowadays the word "Broadway" has come to mean any type of American musical. Sun, Bao-Yin says about the origin and development of Broadway:

> The word Broadway in English denotes a "broad street," which is actually the name of a 25-kilometer long street in central New York that starts at Battery Park and runs from south to north into Manhattan. (2006, p. 30)

Stemming from this street and moving out there lies "Off-Broadway" and "Off-Off-Broadway," two terms which not only represent the outward spreading of the area but also the history of this type of theatrical performance.

From the historical perspective of the American musical, its development was somewhat erratic. It was similar to Chinese traditional Peking opera's performing style of stylization, adding different performance elements at different times to create an entirely new type of musical. In the 1920s, American musicals evolved from a sort of variety entertainment to a combination of script, music, dance, and comedy that included extravagant plots packed with low-end humor and folk songs. The 1960s were a time when the younger generation was anti-tradition and anti-Vietnam War. It was a time when a philosophy and life-style of love and drugs were espoused by the youth, particularly the hippies. The power of music theatrical in the 60s was in fact due to the hippies, and there were also the civil rights and multiple more transparent influences from a range of ethnic groups, and so on. Due to such a liberal mindset, the musical burst forth with variety and amazing creativity.[3]

The contribution of the three elements of dance, drama and song can be based on the director, the playwright, and the actors. A similar example can be taken from the categorization of Chinese operas. Singing opera focuses on song; Kong-Fu opera (做功戲) centers on the posture of martial art; and Romance opera concentrates on reciting monologues (念白戲). The plot of opera gains an advantage through attractive stories. The same similar focus on dance goes for the Broadway musicals. With different ratios of song, dance, and drama, the performances all have their own special characteristics. For example, the core performance of the musical *42nd Street* is tap dance.

---

[3] See Michael Kantor and Laurence Maslon. *Broadway: The American Musical.* New York: Applause, 2010.

The development of musicals is also remarkable. In contemporary society, musicals can be both exquisite and spectacular. The exquisite part includes performances such as: *My Fair Lady*, in which the melody goes through; the anti-narrative in *Sunday in the Park with George*, which features Georges Seurat's neo-impressionism painting "Sunday Afternoon on the Island of La Grande Jatte"; *Chicago*, in which the dark characters are described vividly; *Cat*, which is filled with marvelous dance; and the film *Burlesque* (2010) starring Christina Aguilera and Cher, which revived neo-burlesque with its nightclub dancing and singing. The spectacular part of the musical is exemplified in different ways in several performances including: *Miss Saigon*, in which there is a helicopter; *Phantom of the Opera*, with the gorgeous opera house, the gondola, and the river and cave room underneath; *Les Misérables*, with the tremendous chorus singing and waving of the French flag; *Mamma Mia!* where ABBA's well known song "Dancing Queen" is memorable in the concert scene and impressive in the film starring Meryl Streep. Therefore with the popularity of cultural industries, there is no limitation on musicals being imitated by other drama types as long as "song, dance, drama" is considered as the key element. For example, the composer and musician Elton John collaborated with lyricist Tim Rice to change the opera *Aida* into a musical by adopting the musical melodies of rock and roll and a stage design that represented ancient Egypt. Asian American playwright David Henry Hwang also had thought of the possibility of using a musical to stage a new production about the story of Bruce Lee (premiered in New York, February 2014).

Under the tendency of globalization and the influence of popular culture, the innovation of Hakka opera is toward the translocal style of musicals. Successful musicals in Europe and America may have created this trend. Compared with Mainland China where the original musicals are still in the early phrases of trying to become trendy, Taiwan has promoted and imported musicals from Europe and America for a long time, and local drama troupes and artists, such as Godot Theatre Company, Greenray Theatre, and so on, have learned to produce their own original musicals with increasingly better quality.

SHAKESPEARE ADAPTATION

Taiwan's first Hakka musical, *My Daughter's Wedding*, adopts the style of Broadway musical and, directed by David Jiang from Hong Kong, renovates the traditional Hakka drama. This chapter looks at the way it adapts

Shakespeare's *The Taming of the Shrew* was well as the retheatricalization of the script. I will also scrutinize how this performance reinterprets Hakka culture and Hakka women as the Other, gender roles, and the representation of women in "the male gaze" during the two sexes' power struggle in different eras. I argue that the Hakka theater—evolved from three-role tea drama to Hakka rectified drama and Hakka opera, and then eventually Hakka musical and Hakka opera on TV—reflects the intercultural creativity and innovation of performance in the process of facing Westernization and globalization. Without being limited in the local, Hakka opera goes toward the translocal of psychological marriage anxiety and gender cultural politics, which still prevail in every location of the globe.

HAKKA VERSION

By looking at it in terms of feminism and gender studies we can see how this production adapted Shakespeare's masterpiece while adding the postcolonial perspective of regarding Hakka women as the *Other*. Controversy over the local versus the global can be explored in the Hakka images, the architecture, costumes, and set design of Hsinchu and Meilong and in the local traditional Hakka culture in Kaohsiung, while contrasting global internet online games, heavy motorcycles, and Western Broadway musical theatrical form. Hakka opera is making progress from tradition to innovation.

The content of Hakka opera generally revolves around family ethics, palace life, supernatural or spiritual legends, and more recently there has been an emphasis on investigating the darker side of human nature. For example, in the Hakka performance entitled *Ching-Tien Duan Hsu* (*The Wise Judge Bao, Ching-Tien Ascertains Who's the Real Champion, Prime Minister's Son-in-Law*), the judge needs to work out who's the real champion from the three persons who all claim to be, and the bad guy who tries to gain the champion title by attempting to murder the real one. In contrast to the Hakka, which focuses on culture and ethnic issues, the Western musicals' subject matters consist of an even wider range of topics, which can bring them closer to human beings' everyday lives. There is a particular focus on the theme of love, because "All musical theater embodies the spirit and philosophy of the theater of romance" (Kislan 1995).

In performance style, Hakka opera has a set formula for its music and presentation, whereas the musical does not have restrictions of this kind. Regardless of its chosen subject matter, music, stage design, or style of song and dance, the musical can embrace assorted performing styles and cultural elements. The earlier American Broadway adaptations—such as *Kiss Me, Kate*, an adaptation from Shakespeare's *The Taming of the Shrew*—can be viewed as reference materials to aid in the production of the Hakka musical *My Daughter's Wedding*.

In translocal, the drama genre may break through the local and national boundary by borrowing from Western musical ad incorporating it with Eastern local performing forms. Even though Chinese traditional theater, like Peking opera and *kunqu*, still attracts some certain audience members, Chinese traditional theater is far from becoming a form of mainstream entertainment. By using the musical form, *My Daughter's Wedding* manages to be both popular and artistic, to renovate the traditional Hakka drama and promote the Hakka culture.

In *My Daughter's Wedding* the taming scenario is removed, because it's not suitable for the present day. Instead, Hakka elements are added to depict Hakka legacy and contemporary beliefs about love and marriage. Hakka culture has begun to grow in popularity and the level of traditional Hakka drama performance has risen, opening up a new road for Hakka opera. The intercultural experiment of adapting Shakespeare's *The Taming of the Shrew* in *My Daughter's Wedding* has been combined with the Taiwanese Hakka elements, resulting in innovative, refreshing, and unforgettable enjoyment.

Performance Review

What kind of intercultural theater is produced when Shakespeare's England meets Hakka culture? *My Daughter's Wedding* adopted the style of the Broadway musical, a genre that has grown in popularity in many areas of north east Asia in recent years. The production demonstrated that local artists have gone from importing touring musicals from the West to produce local versions of Western hits with good levels of expertise in dance, music, and design, and so on to creating new musicals with local content. This particular production dealt with gender, power struggles, and marriage anxiety in the context of modern Taiwan and its Hakka traditions.

The script was mainly in Mandarin, but mixed with Hakka, Taiwanese, and English. Linguistically it was meant to appeal to the educated audience on the island, where Mandarin is the official tongue but the other languages mentioned are readily recognized. In ethnicity, Hakka people are more indigenous than Mandarin speakers; the latter are the majority population and the mainstream in culture. The production was directed by

David Jiang from Hong Kong and sponsored by the Council for Hakka Affairs with a budget of approximately $600,000. David Jiang understands both Eastern and Western theater and excels in directing Shakespeare's plays through intercultural theater and Chinese stylization. The council saw this play as a step toward renovating traditional Hakka drama—which originated from Jiang-Hsi Province in China and was imported to Taiwan in 1949, and which has lost its audience—by transforming it into a Hakka musical. As already mentioned, Hakka tea-picking dramas were presented by one actor with one or two actresses and dealt with selling tea. This genre later developed into Hakka opera, which, like other *xiqu*, includes singing, dialogue, mime, and martial arts in stories of history and family morality. But Hakka opera has languished in recent years.

The new work reflected how Chinese artists are seeking to find an innovative intercultural style under the impact of globalization and Westernization to revive local interest. The production was welcomed by most reviewers and the "buzz" in the blogosphere indicated that its efforts to draw youthful audiences toward aspects of traditional Hakka culture were successful. The set (designed by Lu Ping) included a family house full of Hakka characteristics mixed with the Chinese Ming-nan architectural style. The eaves of the house were ornate, showing the family's high status. Hakka symbols such as blue clothes (Fig. 6.1), symbolic of the common Hakka work ethic, and characteristic *tung* blossom designs were appropriated. Hakka blue shirts and pants (with costume design by Lin Ching-Ju) become a symbol of the wife's eventual acceptance of and integration into her traditional role: the women of her husband's family help the Katharina character, Li-Jun, change out of her modern clothes and don this traditional garb. Elements of a traditional wedding ceremony are present, but the new is also evident. There were motorcycles onstage, dancers in sleeveless T-shirts and pants, internet cafés, and modern wedding practices, too.

The play, for audiences, signaled modernity in that it presented Hakka elements in Broadway musical style. The script eliminated the frame story and smoothed over the misogynist tones in Shakespeare's play, successfully transforming the material into a traditional Hakka setting and attracting a large audience.

My Daughter's Wedding was staged by Taipei National University of the Arts, and the cast and stage crew were drawn from the Departments of Theater Arts and Dance. By shifting the theme from the original "taming of a shrew" in Shakespeare's play to "marrying off the daughters," as the

Fig. 6.1 *My Daughter's Wedding* used traditional Hakka dress. (Courtesy of Hakka Affairs Council of Taiwan)

title indicates, the musical reduced the uncomfortable problem of sexism of the original.

Shakespeare's *The Taming of the Shrew* weaves two intertwining story lines— Petruchio's pursuit of Katharina and Lucentio's courting of Bianca—with the story of Sly the tinker used as a framing device. Shakespeare's characters are complex and developed. *My Daughter's Wedding* offers a more linear narrative, diving straight into the main storyline about the taming, cutting Sly's prologue. The characters in the musical were less psychologically developed, but their concerns are more contemporary. Katharina, played by Liou Li-Jun (Hsu Yan-Ling in the première), is a modern new woman, before meeting Petruchio, played by Jong Yo-Jia (Huang Shih-wei). She is direct in showing her contempt for men in her opening speech. Liou Li-Yue (Hung Jui-Hsiang in the première), the younger sister, begins gentle and reserved, but right before her wedding she suddenly demands her personal rights and requests that the prospective groom sign a premarital agreement (a significant alteration from Shakespeare's Bianca). Dance sequences were written into the adaptation to substitute for deleted scenes and connect the narrative.

Only a few portions of Shakespeare's original have been retained. In both Shakespeare's play and the Hakka musical the fathers resolve that "the elder daughter should get married first, and then the younger daughter can get married" as the first premise. Yet in Shakespeare's *The Taming of the Shrew*, Baptista set this rule partly to settle the competitive dispute between his younger daughter's two suitors, Gremio and Hortensio (act 1, scene 1), while in the Hakka musical *My Daughter's Wedding*, Liou Fu-Chung is merely fed up with his daughter Liou Li-Jun's horrible temper and is eager to marry her off first. In both scripts, of course, the leading characters quarrel. For example, in *The Taming of the Shrew*, Katherina and Petruchio are full of wit, sarcasm, and sexual innuendo:

> Katherina: Asses are made to bear, and so are you.
> Petruchio: Women are made to bear, and so are you. (Act 2, Scene 2)
> Compare the above to the following excerpt from *My Daughter's Wedding*:
> Liou Li-Jun: (sing) Asses are for riding, and you are like a stupid ass!
> Jong Yo-Jia: (sing) Women are for riding, and you are a woman!
> Liou Li-Jun: (sing) You wish to ride me? Don't flatter yourself!
> ("Let's Get Matchmaking" in the first act of the show)

The dialogue in Chinese in *My Daughter's Wedding* retains the Shakespearean spirit while also emphasizing the more up-to-date struggle of men and women over power and gender. For instance, the protagonist Jong Yo-Jia says: "I'm strong, and I'm the squad leader in the military service." On the stage, he trains another male dancer to do push-ups, showing a modern manifestation of the patriarchal system—male military culture. The ability to discipline others and sexual capability are implied. Jong Yo-Jia calls himself the "monster squad leader," "all-powerful" competitor, the "hero and king who loves challenges." This iron man knows no such word as "failure," and he views the pursuit of love as a war to win. Met with the superwoman Liou Li-Jun, his dominating manner only draws them further apart. Each lover has a monologue, showing changing attitude and doubts about love.

But by the end of this Hakka musical, the former "shrew," Liou Li-Jun, leans against Jong Yo-Jia, having learned: "The way to a man's heart lies through his stomach." Liou subdues her husband through her culinary gifts, after the need for this "female" skill was pointed out to her in scene 6 by her husband's grandmother: "The secret to couples getting along well is in the kitchen, sharing the ups and downs allows for a long romance. If you share a good fate in this life, you will be able to deal with whatever life throws you!" In the end both sisters and their husbands live happily ever after, and the joyous final chorus song meets audience expectation for a musical comedy's happy ending.

The adaptation of *My Daughter's Wedding* takes its plot largely from the taming part of *The Taming of the Shrew*, mainly focusing on Liou Li-Jun and Jong Yo-Jia, with secondary attention being paid to Liou Li-Yue's romance. This script cuts the play-within-a-play structure to focus on these two intersecting wooings, which unfold in a linear plot.

This particular script cut Shakespeare's prologue and five scenes, simplifying the play to quicken the pace of the story as the narrative mixed up time and space. The lengthy Shakespearean monologues were replaced by lyrical and romantic song solos (music composed by Chien Nan-Chang). There were also a few group chorus pieces (orchestra conductor Chang Chia-Yun). The audience was charmed by the songs intertwined with strong dance choreography (by He Hsiao-Mei) and visually splendid set design (Fig. 6.2) with gorgeous lighting (by Chien Li-Jen).

However, there were weaknesses. The singing and dancing abilities of the leading characters could have been stronger and their Hakka accent more polished. I missed Katherina's controversial reprimand to wives, which was completely left out, perhaps to avoid the deep issues the Shakespearean script poses for a modern audience. The cutting of Sly's framing story eliminated Shakespeare's concepts of dream and reality, performing roles, and playing with words.

This was a successful combination of Shakespeare's play, the traditional Broadway musical, and both modern and Hakka culture. The deconstruction of Shakespeare's frame story and removal of the Elizabethan concept of the patriarchal power allowed for a reinterpretation of gender roles. Modern music and professional dance numbers attracted applause. References to Internet cafés, online gaming, motorcycle machismo, and contemporary military culture made the production up to date, while traditional Hakka elements in set, clothing, female advisement, and wedding customs increased local flavor. The mixture reflected contemporary life and made the work distinctly Taiwanese.

In the following sections, I elaborate further on script adaptation, character comparison, and stage performance, to reveal the significance of this production.

Fig. 6.2 *My Daughter's Wedding*'s production numbers featured modern elements like dancers in T-shirts and with motorcycles. (Courtesy of Hakka Affairs Council of Taiwan)

Translocally, though with the cultural borrowing of Shakespeare's play, cross-over with Taiwanese Hakka customs makes the audiences feel that the local production is more bespoke and relevant. *My Daughter's Wedding* adapts to change the focus from "taming" to "marrying off" to minimize the conflicts between men and women as well as class consciousness. In adaptation, changing the theme from "taming of the shrew" to "marrying off the daughters," allows this Hakka musical to decrease the uncomfortable savage problem found in the original seventeenth-century play. Therefore, the modern perspective in the universal theme of "marrying off the daughters" in this production reverses the blatantly chauvinist undertones in the original Shakespeare's script.

Due to most of the actors speaking in Mandarin, not Hakka language, some people criticize that this work lacks pure or more Hakka elements. However, nowadays few people speak Hakka language. Mandarin is the main official language and English as an international language for the majority of people in Taiwan to communicate in their daily lives. Even some English used in this work can be better understood by audiences than Hakka dialect. Concerning the problem of authenticity in Hakka style, adaptations are done in different countries by different artists creating not just faithful translation but different versions. A so-called "authentic" version of *The Taming of the Shrew* must undergo a redefining, and the flavor of the Hakka dish varies according to the appetite of different cultures. We might adjust flavors to local taste. Thus, the same rationale goes for reserving judgment on an "authentic" Hakka culture.

Analysis of Adaptation Elements

Focusing on the monologues of the female protagonists, the sisters Liou Li-Jun and Liou Li-Yue, I suppose that the anxiety of marriage is the new issue, which the director and the playwright intend to innovate. Women's anxiety about marriage directs the plots. For the male lead protagonist Jong Yo-Jia, this marriage is a challenging and stimulating task. Liou Li-Jun, however, prefers to be celibate. She sings:

> What on earth are the men and how are they able to compare with women? Which thing asks the women to marry? I've never seen such a good thing! In my life, I decide to be celibate!
> ("Here Comes the Spicy Girl" in Act 1)

The transition comes when Liou Li-Jun and Jong Yo-Jia fall in love at first sight. The spotlight focuses on the two, creating a world only for them. A slap breaks through the silent world. The tit for tat between the two is filled with less with the spark of gunpowder but more with unusual chemical flirtation. This is a turning point because Liou Li-Jun agrees to marry Jong Yo-Jia. However, on the eve of the wedding, in contrast to her father's jubilation, the two sisters are very anxious. Though for the shrew Liou Li-Jun, the wedding is her decision, she tries to comfort herself that she is not wrong.

> Liou Li-Jun: (sing) I decide to marry. I decide to marry.
> Though I see him only once, the marriage seems to be destined.
> All men are superficial, but he is with the firm will and his own ideas.
> I am neither deceived by him nor by myself.
> It is settled in a moment, for he and I have made the decision!
> ("The Assembly of Matchmaking" in Act 1)

Liou Li-Jun's mind is changed from being close to reconsidering to now being willing to marry. This stands in contrast to her younger sister Liou Li- Yue, who was wooed by two men but does not know whom she really loves. Li-Yue puts her marriage in the hands of the fate.

> Liou Li- Yue: (sing) Who can have whole heart to me? ...
> Liou Li- Yue: (sing) Facing with dilemmas may change one's mind. ...
> Liou Li- Yue: (sing) Love? Marriage? May the Old Man under the Moon, the Matchmaker God, decide for me
> ("Love Around the Three" in Act 1)

In *My Daughter's Wedding*, the two female characters' attitudes toward marriage reflect the contrast between Li-Jun's active decision making and Li- Yue's passive fate determination.

Later, while not being able to attend her own wedding banquet, Liou Li-Jun is taken rides on a motorcycle with Jong Yo-Jia bound for Meinong, a Hakka village in the south of Taiwan, after being pushed by Jong Yo-Jia to do it. On their way, Li-Jun's luggage, cell phone, and money are lost. Unfortunately, because they do not make it in time to worship the ancestors in the daytime, as called for in the Hakka traditional custom, Li-Jun cannot enter Jong's grandmother's house so she can only sleep in the rice farm. After facing a series of chaotic events, Liou Li-Jun feels confused and in doubt.

This performance points out the uncertainty of a happy marriage. The newlywed couple does not have good communication. Due to her anxiety and concerns, Liou Li-Jun loses her temper. Not sure about Jong's feelings for her, she does not know what to do in the future.

> Liou Li-Jun: (sing) Love, what kind of feeling is it?
> Is it love, so solitude?
> ...
> But I am lost in a mist ocean,
> Do not find the way and do not know where to go?
> ("Seven Cousins-in-Law and Eight Aunts" in Act 1)

Then, immediately, the scene transfers to show her sister Liou Li- Yue in a similar situation of hesitation and worry over their father Fu-Chun's decision to marry her to the wealthy Wu Cheng-Yi. On the stage the two scenes of the sisters' anxiety about marriage juxtaposes with the intersection of space and time. Switching from solo performances, the sisters then have a duet in the mise-en-scène of different dimensions achieved with the juxtaposition of two spotlights on an otherwise black stage. The two sisters sing together in their spotlights about their anxiety, even though they are physically in different places. Although they both have marriage phobia, each finds her answer in temporality.

> Liou Li- Yue: (sing) What on earth makes me be in this kind of situation?
> The saying from the lip seems to be different from the real mind.
> ...
> Who should I choose, who will hold my hand to another side of the red carpet?
> Marriage ah marriage, live with another man
> Will we have many different habits?
> What on earth should I do? What on earth should I do?
> (Jun & Yue) How should I know it is a blissful marriage?
> ...
> (Jun & Yue) From now on, from now on, from single to the couple's world,
> Perhaps after one or two years, children will come to the world,
> My life will be so different,
> Many trials, which I have to overcome with him,
> I will go forward hand in hand with him.
> ("Who Wins the Heart?" Act Two)

Next comes the other wedding of Liou Li- Yue. To everybody's surprise, the tender and timid Li-Yue takes out a premarital agreement and wants Wu Cheng-Yi to sign it before the official marriage ceremony. She wants to guarantee protection of her welfare in the marriage. Similar to Katherina's forty-four-line persuasion monologue after the shrew's transformation in Shakespeare's play, her elder sister Liou Li-Jun attends her younger sister's wedding to lecture about true love.

Liou Li-Jun: (sing) True love occurs between the two,

> We can see through each other's heart and consider for each other,
> True love is not imagination or just sex and appreciation.
> It is that two persons can tolerate, respect, and understand each other in the soul.
> True love is blissful.
> ("The Premarital Agreement" Act Two)

As we know, the two couples live happily ever after and the action ends with a joyful chorus song and a group dance. Although this happy ending fits the standard of most musicals, it is not enough to convince the audience that the superwoman Liou Li-Jun and the male chauvinist Jong Yo-Jia have reached a consensus on how to live their marital lives happily ever after. Or possibly, it is just like the feminism interpretation to the ending of *The Taming of the Shrew* where Katherina's wink at the audience after her long reprimand to the other wives, stresses that everything is only based on performance. By doing so, it can meet the audience's desire to accept the happy ending after they just watched a comical musical and allow them to appreciate the humor. The sensitive taming of the shrew transforms into the happy ending in the local Hakka musical.

A realistic performance such as *My Daughter's Wedding* exposes that the performance on stage is actually mimicking behaviors we see in real life. Furthermore, the stage design and subject matter—that is, parents worrying about their children's marriage—are also realistic. On the stage of realism, the set of a Hakka building is used as a symbol for the unique Hakka religion. The shape of the Liou family house is full of Hakka characteristics mixed with the Chinese Ming-nan architectural style, and the eaves of their house represent the family's authority. This is a contrast to the Hakka village and round tower from Southern Taiwan, which was built according to generation rankings and was designed with war in mind.

Costumes are designed as a pastiche between contemporary fashion and traditional Hakka clothes. The performance places modern and traditional in the same space, such as heavyweight motorcycles, an internet cafe, online games, a traditional wedding ceremony, a modern wedding ceremony, simulation of outdoor banquet, etc. The main language used is Mandarin, mixed with a bit of Hakka, and the speech patterns are also contemporary, therefore the story seems more familiar and easily accessible.

SOCIAL CONSTRUCTION OF HAKKA CULTURE

This performance belongs to the modern style of mimicking realism. Stage performance is displayed as a kind of simulation, as illustrated here.

(1) Conflict and settlement of early translocal immigration

The ethnic conflict that happened during the settlement of early immigrants from China to Taiwan translocally is expressed through the dance fighting simulation movements. In Act 1, the choreography of "Pole Dance" and "Tea-Picking, Sowing Dance" symbolize Hakka immigrants' hardship in cultivating the new land. Martial arts also serve as one of the elements in choreography.

(2) Online games in a virtual reality

The choreographer mimics the gamers' image, concentrative while staring at the screen, and with the fingers jumping quickly across keyboards in the café. Amazingly the avatars of female warriors, the characters of the online game, jump out of the screen from the virtual reality to the real world on the stage. The avatars, played by three dancers in sexy and trendy futuristic robot costumes, appear from the left stage, the right stage, and the middle of the upper stage on the second floor platform, with vigorous postures and shining weapons in their hands like women warriors from another planet. The position of the three is a triangle and it seems like battle among them may be triggered at any moment.

(3) Masculine image presented by military training and physical competitions

Dance to express competition between men is not unusual in ballet or musicals. In this scene, military training style "sit-ups" and "push-ups" and the athletic competitions of "triathlon" and "marathon" are displayed as dance and to show Jong Yo-Jia's enthusiasm for the fights as well as his desire for triumph. It reveals that he is insuperable and has never failed.

(4) Hurry on the way

Immediately after the wedding ceremony, Jong Yo-Jia brutally carries Liou Li-Jun on his shoulder and takes her to Meinong without attending the wedding banquet. In *The Dance of the Motorcycle* the lead female dancer, elegant and slender, dances with the male dancer in a modern ballet style. The dancers' excellent skill is unquestionable. The gentle femininity of the female dancer contrasts with the machinery-like motion of the male dancer. Then there is a big spectacle as a row of about ten Harley Davidson motorcycles astoundingly appear on stage. With the sky projected onto the curtain, it feels and looks just like a group of motorcycles are speeding along the road.

Wedding Preparation

(1) Hakka music and Chinese poetry

In this performance there are two weddings, one in Act 1 and the other in Act 2. The first wedding of Liou Li-Jun has the traditional Hakka music and Chinese poetry. Blessed by all the guests, the musicians are invited to celebrate and bring blessing on the group. The performers bring traditional Chinese musical instruments, such as percussion instruments, and the gift for the bride in their hands. The bride Li-Jun dresses in a red Chinese tight wedding gown to show off her female figure, which symbolizes her spicy temper and joy. In contrast, Li-Yue wears a white Western modern style wedding gown decorated with Western elements, like flower arches and balloons.

(2) Hakka banquet dishes in Meinong

On stage, it is not convenient to present the real banquet in either naturalism nor realism. How will Hakka dishes be presented to the audience? In this performance, accompanied by the singing of Jong's grandmother, the female dancers' movements simulate the presentation of all the dishes. Singing with food ingredients and kitchen utensils displays the feeling of banquet.

Construction of Hakka Culture

(1) Language

The languages used in this performance are Mandarin and Hakka; the screen captions shown are in Mandarin and English. To be specific, in *Four County (Ssu-Hsien)* Hakka dialect is used in this Hakka musical. In addition to serving non-Hakka audiences by using Mandarin and English, the performance can raise the global perspective of Hakka dramas. The ambitions of the Council for Hakka Affairs can be revealed from the selection of the language. However, today's audience cannot completely understand the attractive points of Hakka. Given practical considerations, how many Hakka people nowadays can speak fluent Hakka and understand it? In reality, most Hakka people speak Mandarin and only a few Hakka. Thus, unlike some Hakka scholars who judge the performance by insisting on using only pure Hakka dialect, I think Mandarin, the official language of the populace is legitimate to use in the performance to make sure the meanings are understood by the broad audience members.

(2) Usage of four-line short poetry and jingles

Traditional Hakka four-line short poetry is often used in weddings and celebrations, which must follow the specific rhythm. The sentences are antithesis and there are certain limitations for the rhyming sounds and rhyming words. For example, in the performance the guests Lai and Lan Shi-Ren say the four-line short poems at Liou Li-Jun's wedding, which is used to bless the newly couple.

Lai: The groom and bride are always happy,
The husband and the wife love each other always,
Have a newly born baby soon and with fames,
With fortune and offspring for a hundred million years.
Lan: A round salver blesses the groom and the bride,
Marriage in this good time,
Have a son,
Be a champion next year in life's prime.

In the two four-line short poems, Lai's has an antithesis and *an* (ㄢ) as the rhyme in Chinese. As for Lan's, though it does not follow the format, it can be accepted since the content is festive and easy to read. Four-line short poetry is not specific to Hakka. For the wedding ceremony and celebration in Fujian custom and Taiwanese opera four-line short poetry is also used for blessing and performance.

(3) Songs in Hakka musical

In addition to adding the Chinese poetry rhythm in the lines, Hakka mountain songs are used to show the beautiful Hakka lyrics and scores. In this performance, the Hakka mountain songs sung by the character Lan Shi-Ren (played by Yang Xiu-Heng) show its particular impromptu style. Besides the instrument of tapping, Yang has another traditional musical instrument of "four-plat" holding in his hand, matched with the rhythm for improvisation. Hakka Eight Tunes, one frequent kind of Hakka music creating joyous atmosphere in festivals and celebrations in early Hakka society, are used.

(4) Stage design and Hakka architecture

In the stage design of *My Daughter's Wedding*, Bao Zhong Temple is the Hakka symbol for loyalty. Bao Zhong Temple on stage reminds us of Yi Min Temple in our society in Hsinchu County and Yi Min Festival in Hakka villages. Martial arts and *The Dance of Tea-picking* are in the ceremony of Yi Min Festival. Peng Cheng Hall, the home of the leading character, has Hakka architecture characteristics mixed with Fukienese style as well as a red tiled roof and couplet decorations on the gate.

(5) Hakka dishes

In tourism and the policy of cultural creative industry, Hakka dishes have been popular in recent years. For Hakka people, Hakka dishes are prepared for special occasions, especially the reunion dinner on Chinese New Year and in celebration of good fortunes. Nowadays in the cultural consumption orientation, Hakka dishes have been deritualized to become a kind of commodity. Even non-Hakka people like delicious Hakka dishes. Though the meaning of the dishes has changed, for gourmands the flavor of Hakka dishes is still impressive.

I question whether the blue clothes are a kind of stereotype constructed by social imagination to attribute the invisible Hakka identity. Since few people in the contemporary society speak Hakka dialect, blue clothes serve as the symbol referring to be able to tell who Hakka people are from their appearance. The image of Hakka women is also socially constructed. As Simone de Beauvoir says: "One is not born as a woman, but becomes one." From the perspective of gender performance, under globalization and Westernization, it is hard to distinguish the ethnicity of Taiwanese, Chinese, indigenous, and Hakka women. Therefore in Hakka opera or musical the symbols, such as the blue clothes and white tung flower blossoms, are used as a representation of Hakka culture.

My Daughter's Wedding, because of its musical performance style, shattered conventional dramatic structure of scene division. The narrative and manner of the musical is revolutionary. The production utilizes spontaneity and makes large use of mixing up time and space as well as the real and the virtual. Lengthy Shakespearean monologues have been condensed and replaced by lyrical and romantic songs. The vocals in musicals are limited to large amounts of solos and a few chorus numbers, while refraining from using multiple vocal choruses. What appeals to the audience is the charming, poignant appeal of the songs intertwined with the excellent dance choreography and the visually splendid stage design. Without using the European and American musical structure, in which the play-within-the-play or parallel story structures are often used, the sets in this Hakka musical are changed quickly.

Overall, I think it's proper to choose the intercultural theater—combining the American Broadway musical style and adapting the script from Shakespeare's play along with added Taiwan Hakka cultural elements. Adding Hakka elements increased the local Hakka flavor, and the addition of modernities, professional dance numbers, the deconstruction of Shakespeare's frame story, and the removals of the outdated seventeenth-century Elizabethan concept of the patriarchal power allowed for a reinterpretation of gender roles.

Hakka drama is trying to renovate itself by not only staging Hakka musicals, but also by using other media, like TV, to promote it. The main case analysis of *My Daughter's Wedding* can be embellished referring to the revival of Hakka drama on TV to strengthen the argument that Hakka opera has attempted to move on from traditional Hakka tea-picking drama to become creative theater and TV performances.

Hakka Drama Sin-Yong-Guang Troupe on Hakka TV

After interpreting the Hakka musical, let's talk about the form of Hakka drama on TV. To go beyond the proscenium stage of the theater and the elements of "here" and "live" of theater performing arts, to promote Hakka opera, the media are used to go toward "there" in terms of the translocal performativity. The Council for Hakka Affairs also annually offers funding for Hakka TV stations to broadcast Hakka operas performed by the Hakka troupes, which are chosen from the application auditions. The Hakka drama shown on TV remains the stage performance style. However, in the stage design they have tried to pursue vivid reality. Perhaps learning from the TV Taiwanese opera and TV puppet theater, which have been produced and shown on TV for many years, Hakka drama shown by Hakka TV stations can improve.

Taking the example of the Sin-Yong-Guang Troupe, which have been performing Hakka drama on a Hakka TV station from 2003 up to the present, most of the troupe's productions are about loyalty, filial piety, fidelity, and righteousness. They shoot and record the stage performance in the indoor proscenium theater in Taipei County, so their performance is for the viewers to watch on TV after they edit the actors' stage performances. There are a number of differences between the live performance and the edited TV program that is aired. First, the TV station director decides which camera shot among the three TV cameras will be chosen to be edited to create the sequence and then the whole drama program. Second, every move and action of the actors must follow the script and the director's indication, to be sure that the three TV cameras get the best shots. Third, the content of the plot concentrates on the characters, aided by the love story, in a linear development and cuts the minor details. Fourth, every five series create a drama program; among the five, the previous four are descriptions of the story and only the last one is the climax and the ending. In the denouement, most have a happy ending.

The stage design is mostly drawings in the background on hard wooden boards matched with soft drapes. Most of the scenery design includes the interior decoration, screens with drawings of orchid or peony, artificial mountains, ponds, a pavilion in the garden scene, mountains in the wilderness, and so on. Some troupes help performers to rent or borrow costumes. Hair decorations are what the actresses provide themselves. The cast is in colorful costumes to be presented as a visually splendid spectacle on TV.

The Yang's Ninth Sister

Using one TV Hakka opera as an example, *The Yang's Ninth Sister* (2009) was shot on August 25, 2009 in the Hakka Cultural Park in Taipei County and shown on TV from 6:30 pm to 7:00 pm on November 2–6, 2009. (Fig. 6.3) The exploration of the aspects of the script, casting, deficiency of performers, and representation on TV are discussed in the following.

Scrutinizing the history and adaptation change of Hakka opera, in *A Theory of Adaptation*, Linda Hutcheon indicates six factors for us to consider—"What, Who, Why, How, Where and When" (2006, p. 1). Most of the Hakka scripts are either from the oral tradition, passing from the old performers to the next young generation of performers, or transplanted from the other drama categories such as Taiwanese opera, or Chinese Peking opera, and then adapted into Hakka dialect or performed on the outdoor stage opera repertory. Lee, Cheng-Kuang was inspired by the Fujian opera in China to write the script of *The Yang's Ninth Sister*. Actually, the Yang family generals' stories are well known tales from history. In opera, the representative ones are *The Yang's Fourth Son Visits*

Fig. 6.3 *The Yang's Ninth Sister*, Hakka TV drama, is performed by Sin-Yong-Guang Troupe. (Courtesy of Hakka Affairs Council of Taiwan)

Mother, Mu, Kuei-Yin as the Commander in Chief, and so on. The drama stories related to the golden knife are most concerned with the Yang's eighth sister. This is the first time that the Hakka drama uses the Yang's ninth sister as the protagonist.

It is a pity that the script does not follow the title of how the Yang's ninth sister makes use of her wisdom to acquire the golden knife in a complex dramatic development and praise her accomplishment, but rather is just a flat description of the story. The plot begins with the battle at the white sand beach where Old General Yang and almost all his seven sons (except his fifth son who became a monk and retreated to the mountain) die heroically. The enemy Liao Country, a Chin minority race that inhabited the north, grabbed Old General Yang's miraculous golden knife to use as a powerful weapon during a war with the Han race in the Song Dynasty in Chinese history. The prime minister advised the Chinese emperor to invite Madame She, Old General Yang's wife, to lead the fight.

The Yang's ninth sister, in order to solve the problem for her mom, for the benefit of her country, and for her family's legacy, decides to masquerade as a man and bravely go by herself into the enemy camp to get her father's golden knife back. Yet, in her male masquerade, the princess Chin-Lien of Liao Country falls in love with him/her. They get engaged and, with the help of the princess, the Yang's ninth sister gets back the golden knife successfully.

However, in my view, this performance script has neither the tragedy of *The Yang's Fourth Son Visits Mother* nor the grandiose of *Hwa, Mu-Lan's Substitute for Father to Go to the Army*. The adaptation of this script is out of focus and the details could have been more specific. The playwright might have been able to improve it. For example, instead of just using the strategy of masquerading, arranging the meeting with Yang, Tzung-Bao, her elder brother who was found alive, and the subsequent steps of fighting in the war, the scriptwriting should have strengthened the focus on following the logic of using "wisdom to get the golden knife." During the process of script adaptation, the logical rationality and the retheatricalization of the words on stage should be paid very close attention.

Choosing the right performers is important. In my observations during the rehearsal process, the cast has a problem. In modern performance on stage, on TV, and in the cinema in Taiwan, they choose convincing and capable performers based upon appearance, age, and expertise. Yet in traditional opera, they care more about the type of roles the performers are good at and their years of training. However, facing the new photographic technology, any facial expression or fluid body movement can be detected so clearly. The camera, especially close shots, works like an enlarged mirror and the viewer can see the wrinkles clearly even if they are covered by make-up. Therefore, it is not convincing for the viewers to watch the roles of Yang, Ten-Integrity, and the young Yang's ninth sister being played by the same old fat actress who is then able to win the beautiful young princess's heart. Once presented on the camera, the lines of the handsome young male role do not fit with the female performer's image, which makes it hard for the audiences to believe it. It is not only the protagonist but also the supporting roles, such as the soldiers, that are all played by the old performers, who are mostly female. How can they really show that they are a strong army who can fight and win the war?

It is necessary to be more exquisite, no matter whether in writing the content of the script, designing props and costumes, or finding a cast who fit with the TV photographic technology more appropriately. The picture in the camera's close-up shot speaks loudly to the audiences. As the saying goes "A picture is worth a thousand words," so if the picture does not match what the audience expects then, no matter how well acted the performance, they will not believe it and lose interest. Take the TV Idol Soap Opera produced by Taiwan, Japan, and Korea for example. They get young handsome actors and beautiful actresses who perform well to be the protagonists so they can attract larger audiences to watch the TV programs, thus raising the viewing ratio and gaining more interest from commercials, which in turn generates more income. Then how come the TV Hakka opera has the problem of old performers playing the teenager and young roles?

I discovered that there are three reasons. First, there is the trouble of having no young talented performers in Hakka drama. Essentially there is an old age problem. It is still the biggest problem Hakka opera faces when it tries to promote itself and attract an audience nowadays. Second, there is the right to perform and the name needed to get funding. Although it is Sin-Yong-Guang Troupe who gets the right and chance to perform and have a show on TV, two thirds of the performers are supported by the other troupe, De-Tai Troupe. Perhaps the guest troupe of De-Tai Troupe respects the right of the master troupe of Sin-Young Guang Troupe so they assign some of the major roles to the old performers of Sin-Young Guang Troupe to prove that Sin-Young Guang Troupe who applied for the project and got the funding really participated in this performance. Third, maybe there is no capable actress who has enough training in De-Tai Troupe to play the lead roles. Thus, in assigning the roles, there is such a contrast between young beautiful actresses who are not well trained enough and older actresses who are well trained but do not fit the right look for the performance. This problem can be directly attributed to lack the young talent in Hakka opera.

In relation to performing method in performance studies, overall, the performers are family members so they support each other when they demonstrate their skills. The costumes and make-up of Hakka opera imitate the Chinese opera. The details of the Hakka costumes could be more calculated. Nonetheless, TV Hakka soap opera still has merits, including showing particular Hakka wedding customs, tea-picking tools, Hakka clothes, rules of celebrating Chinese New Year, and so on, to show Hakka culture. The stage director's mise-en-scène can make use of the whole stage space, instead of just using the center and middle upstage. The large setting can be better used than just serving as the place-changing function. It is good to have enough lighting; there are nine lights up in the air for the stage, some footlights in the front stage, and the two rows of bright lights, like the small-scale lights in the football stadium, each down by the stage right and left before the auditorium. The TV station director did a good job of not just examining the multiple TV screens for good angles, but also supervising the whole fluid performance, including checking the make-up, lines, and movement.

With improvisation, in Hakka traditional opera, performers can still reserve the creative space for improvisation and do not need to just follow the script. The old actress who plays the lead role embellishes the singing and movement stylizations by pausing or lengthening the tone to deepen the meaning of sub-text, which is not written in the script. TV uses three cameras to capture the other performers' facial expressions and actions to aid with choosing the edits to make the script not just for reading as literature but also for performing.

The stage director keeps the stylization and fighting scenes with Hakka opera props of long guns and long sticks to present the traditional stylization of Hakka opera heritage while adding the modern performing movements. However, stage design, costume choice, performer numbers, and the deployment of performers' actions should be more careful to match up with the lines without any conflict with the script descriptions. In this TV Hakka opera, the TV director employs several kinds of shots, such as whole shot, far-away shot, close-shot, zoom-in, zoom-out, fade-in, fade-out, and so on, to have a variety on the screen. Some errors, like synchronizing the image and sound, can be fixed before the program is broadcast on TV in the post-editing checking process.

Briefly analyzing the abovementioned results, first, in regards to the script we may adopt Hutcheon's theory of adaptation to consider the 5W and 1H to pay attention to the logical arrangement and story adaptation into the performance script. Second, choosing the cast should be based upon the characters described in the play. Suitable performers should be chosen to convince the audiences so that the performance can achieve double the success with half the efforts. Third, improve the deficiency of Hakka performers results in several traditional Hakka troupes' cooperation on the production. Fourth, considering the aesthetics of TV media, there is a necessity to solve the problem of old-aged performers playing young roles on TV, especially during the close-up shots. Fifth, the setting background and performers' make-up, hairdos, and costumes need to match with what the script lines say. Finally, it is important to synchronize the images and sounds and carefully fix those problems in post-editing.

CONCLUSION

Trans the geographies and temporalities from China to Taiwan, Hakka three-role tea-picking opera in Taiwan has gradually developed into Hakka rectified opera and Hakka opera, such as *Wu Tang-Hsing*, produced by Cheng, Jung-Hsing Hakka Troupe, about the title Hakka hero fighting in Japanese colonialization, performed in the theater of Taipei City Hall. It was the first Hakka musical produced in accordance with the advance of time and the change of audiences' tastes. This chapter focuses on *My Daughter's Wedding*, a Hakka musical in Taiwan adapted from Shakespeare's *The Taming of the Shrew*, and refers to *The Yang's Ninth Sister*, a Hakka drama performed by the Sin-Yong-Guang Troupe and played on TV. The issues of ethnicity and identity are explored to discover the process and draw the conclusion about Hakka opera's shifting from tradition to creation.

To renovate Hakka opera, in cultural policy, I'd like to suggest some improvement strategies for the government and related cultural, media, and art organizations, like the Ministry of Culture, National Culture and Arts Foundation, TV stations, National Theater, and so on. First, create a system that allocates funding to schedule an art training program where the senior performers can teach the young generation the stylization, singing, and acting of Hakka opera. Second, theater, as one of our cultural creative industries, may link with TV and cinema. Take the reference of the Globe Theatre and Royal Shakespeare Company in England, see how they manage to make use of Shakespeare's cultural legacy in the seventeenth century so that it is still popular in the twentieth-first century to tour their classical performances around the world. Research the cultural studies in the phenomenon of popular culture and entertainment programs, like pop songs, dance, talent shows, model shows, and Korea's packaging and marketing of singers such as Girls' Generation and K-Drama shown by Roku in the US, as well as the global popularity of European and American singers and bands today. Taiwan needs to find ways for young people to have motivation and willingness to learn Hakka opera and to have the chances to perform it as a career. Third, recruit the best specialists in each field, like playwrights, performers, stage directors, TV directors, marketing managers, and so on, to create the unique Hakka opera with Eastern flavor and a good Taiwan brand.

This first Hakka musical, *My Daughter's Wedding*, has successfully altered the traditional style of the Hakka drama by attracting audiences to view this production at the National Theater and other major cultural centers. This innovative Hakka play was performed in the style of a Broadway musical and adapted from Shakespeare's *The Taming of the Shrew*. It recreated the Hakka legacy using contemporary views on love and marriage. The musical has become a trendy pastime for audiences pursuing classy entertainment in a metropolitan, commercialized society with popular culture. Under the influence of globalization, Hakka drama has been renovated by the sponsorship of the Council for Hakka Affairs, which spent a lot of money inviting professionals from all around the globe to accomplish the first Hakka musical *My Daughter's Wedding* and Hakka TV drama series.

The movement to spread Hakka culture proved effective and traditional Hakka plays are once more enjoying time in the spotlight. The combination of Eastern elements and Western performance style and script, in addition to the support of the Council for Hakka Affairs and the cooperation of those talented artists, reversed the reclusive attitude most Hakka held about their identities and brought the issue to light. The Hakka musical *My Daughter's Wedding* and Hakka opera shown on TV have successfully paved a new way for Hakka drama, going across the translocal by singing and dancing across the boundaries of the Hakka ethnicity to speak to a broad audience.

I find there is cultural mobility. In *Modernity at Large: Cultural Dimensions of Globalization* Arjun Appadurai advocates for "a new postnational discourse and an anthropology that captures the qualities of translocal culture" (Appadurai 1996, p. 1411). In the contemporary world, the local Hakka culture might transmit to the different locations in globalization and have some changes after the influence and reception of translocal culture. Through the government's sponsorship and cultural policy, let's make the production of the Hakka opera production locality flow. Through innovative script adaptation and creation of theatricality, after change and transformation, the local ethnic Hakka opera can one day have aesthetic mobility with cultural glocalization, to go across boundaries, imbuing with translocal culture.

BIBLIOGRAPHY

Albrow, Martin. "Modernity at Large: Cultural Dimensions of Globalization by Arjun Appadurai." *American Journal of Sociology*, 103(5): March 1998, pp. 1411–1412.

Appadurai, Arjun. *Modernity at Large: Cultural Dimensions of Globalization*. Minneapolis: University of Minnesota Press, 1996.

Baudrillard, Jean. 2008. "Simulation." *Performance Studies.* Ed. Richard Schechner, 117–123.
Crocker, Holly A. (Holly Adryan) 2003. "Affective Resistance: Performing Passivity and Playing A-Part in *The Taming of the Shrew.*" *Shakespeare Quarterly,* 54(2): 142–159.
Huston, J. Dennis. 1967. "To Make a Puppet." *Shakespeare Studies,* vol. 9: 73, p. 15.
Hutcheon, Linda. *A Theory of Adaptation.* New York and London: Routledge, 2006.
Kislan, Richard. 1995. "The Musical: A Look at American Musical Theater." British Library Cataloging—in- Publication.
Krims, Marvin B. 2002. "Uncovering hate in The Taming of the Shrew" *Sexuality & Culture* 6.2: 49–64.
Lichte, Fischer Erika. 2003. "Quo Vadis? Theatre Studies at the Crossroads." *Theatre Journal,* 48–66.
Maguire, Laurie E. 1997. "Culture Control in *Taming of the Shrew.*" Rose, Marry B. ed. *Renaissance Drama*: New Series XXVI. Northwestern University Press, 1995, 83–105.

Chinese Materials

Creation Volume of A New Hakka Musical: My Daughter's Wedding. Taipei: Council for Hakka Affairs, 2008.
Editing and Commentaries of A New Hakka Musical: My Daughter's Wedding. Taipei: Council for Hakka Affairs, 2008.
Wang, Jun Ting. "Discussion on the Development of Taiwan Musicals Based on the Western Musical's History and Characteristics." (〈從西方音樂劇的歷史與特質看台灣音樂劇的發展〉) *Taiwan University of Arts* 78 (《藝術學報》) (2006): 165–183.
Chu, Chi-Tien. "The Shaming of the Shrew: the Tricks Taught in the Taming-School." (〈奴顏婢膝:御妻學校中傳授的馴悍秘訣〉) *Journal of Humanities College of Liberal Arts National Chung Hsing University* 37 (2006): 365–379.
Chu, Vivian Ching-Mei. "Sondheim/Prince's "Concept Musical": Creative Methods and Process." (〈桑坦/普林斯的"概念音樂劇"創作方法之研究〉) *International Conference On Performance Art.* (2004).
Lu Chien Chung. "The Virtual Courtship Dance: Comment On the Royal Shakespeare Company's *Taming of the Shrew.*" (<虛擬求偶舞-評英國皇家莎士比亞劇團《馴悍記》>) *Performance Art* 92 (《表演藝術》) (2000): 67–69.
Li Chiu Min. "The Musical *Aida*: Rock Fashion and Full of Youth"〈歌舞劇《阿伊達》搖滾時尚洋溢青春〉, *Performance Art Review* 191(《表演藝術雜誌》) (2008): 10–11.

Lin, Alan Ying-nan (林境南). "Style and Interpretation: Feeling of *Hamlet* and *The Taming Of The Shrew.*" (〈風格與詮釋-看《哈姆雷特》與《馴悍記》有感〉) *Performance Art* 92(《表演藝術》) (2000): 62–65.

Chu, Chi Hung. "Musical and the Contemporary Stage Revolution of Our Country." (〈音乐剧与我国当代舞台变革〉) *Yellow Bells* 4(《黃鐘》) (2008): 107–114.

Chiu, Yuan. "From 'Musical Comedy' To 'Musical'." (〈從「音樂喜劇」到「音樂劇」〉) *Music Monthly* 120 (《音樂月刊》) (1994): 140–114.

Keng, Yi Wei (耿一偉). "It's Successful to Make the Audience Laugh: Shakespeare's comedy and The Contemporary Production." (〈但能博得觀眾喜,便是功成圓滿時—莎士比亞喜劇與當代製作〉) *Performance Art Review* 191 (《表演藝術雜誌》) (November 2008): 81–85.

Sun, Pao Yin. "Theatre In Broadway."〈百老匯戏剧面面观〉, *Contemporary Theatre* 1 (《當代戲劇》) (2006): 30–31.

Yeh Ken Chuan. "*My Daughter's Wedding*: This Hakka Dish is not tasty." (〈《福春嫁女》-一道不入味的客家小炒〉) *Academic Journal of Theatre Dept., National Taiwan University of Arts* 7 (《戲劇學刊》) (2008): 241–243.

Yu, Hsiu Li. "Talking About the Broadway Musicals." (〈漫談百老匯音樂劇〉) *Youth Monthly* 359 (《幼獅月刊》) (1980): 56–57.

Lei, Bi-qi (雷碧琦). "Androgynous In Shakespeare's Comedies." (〈既女又男戲扮裝,玩趣背後破藩籬—莎士比亞喜劇中的雌雄同體〉)*Performance Art Review* 191 (《表演藝術雜誌》) (2008): 88–89.

Hsieh, Camilla Chun-pai (謝君白) "The Strategy to Tame the "Taming of the Shrew": Text and Performance Observation." (〈馴服《馴悍記》的策略:文本與表演的觀察〉) *Chung-Wei Literary Monthly* 28, no. 9 (《中外文學》) (2000): 86–118.

Websites

Project of Culture and Creative Products (文化創意產業計畫) http://web.cca.gov.tw/creative/page/main_03.htm/2008/08/25

Yu, Shan Lu. (于善祿). Comment On the New Hakka Musical *My Daughter's Wedding* (<評新客家歌舞劇《福春嫁女》>) 2007.11.03. http://mypaper.pchome.com.tw/news/yushanlu/3/1297921354/20071103012940/2008/03/25

Others

Program of a New Hakka Musical: *My Daughter's Wedding*. 2008.
R'Way Broadway: The American Musical. Well Go USA. Inc, 2004.

Video-Audio Materials

My Daughter's Wedding. 2DVDs. Taipei: Council for Hakka Affairs. 2008.
My Daughter's Wedding. 2CDs. Taipei: Council for Hakka Affairs. 2008.
R'Way Broadway: The American Musical Explores the 100-Year History and Evolution of American Art Form. 3DVDs. Well Go USA. Inc. 2004.

Interview

Iris Hsin-chun Tuan. Interviewed Director Jiang Wei-Kuo twice. Taipei. Taipei University of the Arts and National Theatre. Oct. 2007.

CHAPTER 7

Hakka Culture and Image in Film and Performance

Abstract Performing Hakka culture and images on screen and stage is explored by the three case studies—the movie *China My Native Land* (1980), Neo-Classic Dance Company's "The Drifting Fate of Hakka," (December 5–7, 2014, Taipei National Theater), and the music concert representing Chung Lihe (1915–1960)'s short novel to present aesthetics of simplicity, cultural mobility, love, and belongingness. In the movie, Hakka culture and image are represented by theatrical cinematography. In the dance performance, choreographer Lu, Yi-Chuan uses dance to portray Hakka immigrants' ethnicity history in the global scope. In the music concert "Belongingness in Heart is Your Native Land" (October 24, 2015, Taipei), Composer Chou created the music scores and collaborated with three dancers. Hakka culture and image are visualized by the aesthetics of minimalism.

Keywords "The Drifting Fate of Hakka" • Chung Lihe (鍾理和)
• *My Native Land* • Cultural mobility

INTRODUCTION

Hakka ethnicity as a minority used to be invisible; with the Democratic Progressive Party (DPP)'s political policy and change over time, Hakka culture and Hakka people are more emphasized than before. In the theoretical frame of cultural mobility and translocality, I argue that Hakka culture can be spread and dissimilated by cinema and live performances as the interesting media for the purpose of education and entertainment. Performing Hakka culture and images on screen and on stage is explored by the three case studies in this chapter: the movie *China My Native Land*《原鄉人》(1980), Neo-Classic Dance Company's "The Drifting Fate of Hakka" (2014), and the music concert (2015) representing Chung Lihe (鍾理和, 1915–1960)'s short novel.

Cultural Mobility

Using Stephen Greenblatt's *Cultural Mobility: A Manifesto* to examine Hakka culture, cultures, "even traditional cultures are rarely stable or fixed" (Greenblatt 2005). In the vein of this thinking, although Hakka culture may be regarded as a traditional culture, it is neither stable nor fixed so it can be innovated and Hakka images can be improved.

> First, *mobility must be taken in a highly literal sense.*
> Second, *mobility studies should shed light on hidden as well as conspicuous movements* of peoples, objects, images, texts, and ideas.
> Third, *mobility studies should identify and analyze the "contact zones" where cultural goods are exchanged.*
> Fourth, *mobility studies should account in new ways for the tension between individual agency and structural constraint.*
> Fifth, *mobility studies should analyze the sensation of rootedness.*
> (Greenblatt 2010: 250–253)

Mobility—that is, the ability to move or be moved freely— has a high status, with the movements of people, concepts, commodities, works, and images. In the contact zones, cultural products are exchanged. It goes without saying, there is a tension between individual freedom and structure limitation. In mobility studies, we are still drawn toward the source. While we look forward to Hakka new modern images, we still look back to the deep roots of Hakka tradition. Therefore the three case studies in this chapter are roughly divided into the traditional and the modern. Looking back of Hakka tradition, the movie *My Native Land* is the example of Hakka deep-rootedness. The other case studies—Neo-Classic Dance Company's "The Drifting Fate of Hakka" (2014) and the music concert "Belongingness in Heart is Your Native Land" (2015)—are the examples of modern Hakka images representing Hakka culture.

Echoing Greenblatt's second idea, the flows of people and information are related to translocality. Just as Arjun Appadurai indicates: "The many displaced, deterritorialized, and transient populations that constitute today's ethnos capes are engaged in the construction of locality." (1996, p. 199) Examining the relationship among the dimensions of global cultural flows, further refracting these disjunctures are what Appadurai call *mediascapes* and *ideoscapes*, "which are closely related landscapes of images" (p. 35). Ideas flow in landscapes. Hakka images can spread across the world from one location to the other. The ideas and culture of Hakka can be conveyed via cinema and performances.

CASE STUDIES

The Movie My Native Land

The film *My Native Land* is a drama directed by Lee Hsing (Fig. 7.1). Adapted from the novel of the same name by Hakka writer Chung Lihe, the topic of this autobiographical film is marriage. We see Hakka culture

Fig. 7.1 Film poster of *My Native Land*. Retrieved from www.city.fukuoka.lg. jp (Courtesy of Lee Hsing)

and image represented through cinematography. The film depicts the story of Chung Lihe (1915–1960), the Hakka writer born in Pingtung, and his career while living under Japanese colonialization (1895–1945). The film is shot in linear narrative. Chung Lihe falls in love with Chung, Tai-Mei, who works in Chung's farm. However, as Hakka traditional custom at the time forbids marriage to someone with the same last name, they elope via Japan to Shenyang in north east China. After Chung, Tai-Mei gives birth, they return to live in Meinung in southern Taiwan. Chung dedicated himself to writing continuously all day. After returning to Taiwan, unfortunately, he got lung disease and was tortured by it until he died at the young age of forty-five. Chung insisted on love and on writing. In the short novel *My Native Land*, he describes his longing for and nostalgia toward the ideal native land.

Through close-up shots, we can see the handsome and resolute facial expression of Chung Lihe (played by the attractive male lead Chun Hon) and the shy and pretty face of Chung, Tai-Mei (played by the beautiful female lead Joan Lin Feng-Jiao). In the beginning of the film, there are eight minutes of pretty scenery during a train ride. The viewer is captivated as the protagonists smile at each other while the snow fields pass behind them and a stunning song is sung by Teresa Li-Chun Teng.

Slow motion camera shots highlight the beautiful layers of green tea fields along the mountain edges for our viewing pleasure. Through Chung, Tai-Mei's hard work picking tea leaves, weaving shoe boxes, cultivating the land, cutting wood, and so on, we get a glimpse into what Hakka people's tough daily lives were like in the past. The melodramatic acting of both the lead actor and actress arouses the viewers' sympathy. Through Chun's good acting we observe the legendary Chung's dedication to writing even while suffering with lung cancer. The film demonstrates his persistence—he died at his desk while still writing in blood— and this image of him as the "Writer Who Falls upon Blood" is imprinted in the film and our mind. In memory Chung's short yet memorable forty-five years, this film keeps a historical record of Hakka culture, Hakka intellectual, and Hakka hardworking images in cinema.

Neo-Classic Dance Company's "The Drifting Fate of Hakka"

Neo-Classic Dance Company's "The Drifting Fate of Hakka" (December 5–7, 2014, Taipei National Theater), choreographed by Lu, Yi-Chuan, uses dance to portray Hakka immigrants' ethnic history in the global sphere. It combines traditional rituals and modern dance. Lu, from the perspective of history, literature, and philosophy, shows visually rather than through narrative the "reverse-the-wind spirit of Hakka ethnicity in the process of constant immigration."[1] As well as the dancing, this Hakka dance performance also adopts storytelling and singing to add theatricality. (Fig. 7.2) It combines modern ballet and modern dance with classical Chinese dance, folk dance, Kung-Fu, and so on to tell the touching story of Hakka immigrants.

Like migrant birds, Hakka people had migrated from China to Taiwan, from the plain to the mountain. Using tea-picking dance and movement, this performance recalls the past Hakka traditions and way of living to enable the audience members to imagine what the Hakka were like in the agricultural time. Incorporating Hakka old mountain songs, Hakka small tunes, rituals, and eight yiwn dance, the dancers and the singers together weave good and simple Hakka images and touching Hakka songs in the live stage performance (Fig. 7.3).

Fig. 7.2 The dancers dance while the singers sing a duet on the roof to celebrate Hakka community lives. (Courtesy of Neo-Classic Dance Company)

[1] The introduction of this piece in Chinese in *PAR*. http://par.npac-ntch.org/article/show/1414999923366375.

Fig. 7.3 The dancers dance well and the singers sing touching Hakka songs. Together they weave a good and simple picture of that earlier Hakka agricultural time in the live stage performance. (Courtesy of Neo-Classic Dance Company)

Rooted in Chinese nationalism and culture, choreographer Lu, following artistic director Liu Feng-Hseuh's idea, transforms and recreates Chinese dance by adding Hakka culture. In the perspective of history, culture, humanity, and philosophy, the dance performance "The Drifting Fate of Hakka" extends ethnic immigration, just like bird migration, to delineate the life process. The performers consist of Neo-Classic Dance Company, Team Win Lion Dance Theatre, and the Department of Acrobatics at National Taiwan College of Performing Arts. Neo-Classic Dance Company collaborates with composer Li He-Pu, singer Hsieh Yu-Wei, and a top artistic team to present this visual and aural Hakka dance performance, a fusion of tradition and modernity.

The Music Concert "Belongingness in Heart is Your Native Land"

The music concert "Belongingness in Heart is Your Native Land" (October 24, 2015, Taipei), performed in the Taipei City Hakka Music Theater Center, retells Chung's story. The music concert is based on combines traditional rituals and modern dance. Lu, from the perspective of history, literature, and philosophy, shows visually rather than through narrative the "reverse-the-wind spirit of Hakka ethnicity in the process of constant immigration."[1] As well as the dancing, this Hakka dance performance also adopts storytelling and singing to add theatricality. (Fig. 7.2) It combines modern ballet and modern dance with classical Chinese dance, folk dance, Kung-Fu, and so on to tell the touching story of Hakka immigrants.

Like migrant birds, Hakka people had migrated from China to Taiwan, from the plain to the mountain. Using tea-picking dance and movement, this performance recalls the past Hakka traditions and way of living to enable the audience members to imagine what the Hakka were like in the agricultural time. Incorporating Hakka old mountain songs, Hakka small tunes, rituals, and eight yiwu dance, the dancers and the singers together weave good and simple Hakka images and touching Hakka songs in the live stage performance (Fig. 7.3).

Fig. 7.2 The dancers dance while the singers sing a duet on the roof to celebrate Hakka community lives. (Courtesy of Neo-Classic Dance Company)

[1] The introduction of this piece in Chinese in *PAR*. http://par.npac-ntch.org/article/show/1414999923366375.

Fig. 7.3 The dancers dance well and the singers sing touching Hakka songs. Together they weave a good and simple picture of that earlier Hakka agricultural time in the live stage performance. (Courtesy of Neo-Classic Dance Company)

Rooted in Chinese nationalism and culture, choreographer Lu, following artistic director Liu Feng-Hseuh's idea, transforms and recreates Chinese dance by adding Hakka culture. In the perspective of history, culture, humanity, and philosophy, the dance performance "The Drifting Fate of Hakka" extends ethnic immigration, just like bird migration, to delineate the life process. The performers consist of Neo-Classic Dance Company, Team Win Lion Dance Theatre, and the Department of Acrobatics at National Taiwan College of Performing Arts. Neo-Classic Dance Company collaborates with composer Li He-Pu, singer Hsieh Yu-Wei, and a top artistic team to present this visual and aural Hakka dance performance, a fusion of tradition and modernity.

The Music Concert "Belongingness in Heart is Your Native Land"

The music concert "Belongingness in Heart is Your Native Land" (October 24, 2015, Taipei), performed in the Taipei City Hakka Music Theater Center, retells Chung's story. The music concert is based on

Chung's short novel, presenting aesthetics of simplicity, cultural mobility, love, and belongingness. Composer Chou created the music scores to collaborate with the three dancers from Legend Lin Dance Theatre (無垢舞團). The result is a cross-boundary inter-disciplinary performance combining music and dance.

Artistic director Lin Huan-Ling created the short song "Fall in Love" based on Chung's love story. The music was performed by the String Orchestra, who created an abundant musical sound effect. Moreover, clarinet musician Chuang Kai-wei was invited to play a graceful jazz piece by American composer Aaron Copland, rarely performed in Taiwan. The sound resonates well in the theater. From this music concert, Hakka novels, and literature of Chung's contributions to culture are visible, and the Hakka image of Chung's persistence in love and writing is recalled and remembered.

Chung demonstrated his amazing commitment to love and writing no matter what difficulties and hardship he encountered. His spirit is admired by us. The hero's image as a good person who sticks to his ideal of love and writing can be seen not just in Hakka ethnicity, but also in all human beings.

The case studies in this chapter display Hakka culture and images in cinema and theater performing arts (dance and concert).

Translocality

I argue that we can extend from Greenblatt's notion of cultural mobility to translocal studies and my invention of translocality. Gregory Doran's book *Shakespeare's Lost Play: In Search of Cardenio*, shows the Hakka opera *Betrayal* as representing Taiwan's translocal version, performing Hakka images through the aesthetics of simplicity in minimalism. I argue that Hakka culture and images are represented by theatricality in cinema and performances to show Hakka ethnicity, immigration, belongingness via cultural mobility, and translocality. In the process of glocalization, cultures are translocalized to enhance the rich treasure of theater performing arts.

Conclusion

The good Hakka images are irresistible. So why resist? Why not keep Hakka culture and remember Hakka images in cinema and live performances as they are efficient methods of education and entertainment?

While theatrical mobility may exist in different adaptations, glocalization can integrate translocal cultures and theatrical performing methods. The issues of Hakka culture and Hakka images are explored in terms of cultural mobility and translocality in this chapter. Hakka culture and images can be visibly seen in cinema and the live performances of drama, dance, and music.

Given the provenance of theater as a cultural laboratory, in a way it operates a repository for diverse histories and is significant as a site for dialogue. With the development of pristinc narratives in the translocal e-era, we see the relevance of theater and performance studies becoming as important as film study research. Theater acts as an artistic laboratory for understanding historical and socio background that embeds Asian identities. Cultural exchange and commercial transactions bring together the indigenous and the transnational, the local and the global, and the performative and the cinematic performance are intertwined in translocaity.

BIBLIOGRAPHY

Barranger, Milly S. 2004. *Understanding Plays*, 3rd ed. U.S.A.: Pearson Education Editions.

Bhabha, Homi. 1987. "Of Mimicry and Man: The Ambivalence of Colonial Discourse." In *October*, edited by Joan, Douglas Crimp, Rosalind Krauss & Annette Michelson, 317–325. Cambridge: MIT Press.

Bharucha, Rustom. 2002. "Interculturalism and Multiculturalism in an Age of Globalization: Discriminations, Discontents, and Dialogue." In *The Color of Theatre*, edited by Roberta Uno and Lucy Mae San Pablo Buns, 27–38. London and New York: Continuum.

Baudrillard, Jean. "Feigning to Have What One Doesn't." Performativity. Ed. Richard Schechner. *Performance Studies: An Introduction*. London and New York: Routledge, 2002.

Foucault, Michel. *Discipline and Punish: The Birth of the Prison*. Trans. Alan Sheridan. New York: Vintage, 1977.

Greenblatt, Stephen. *Renaissance Self-Fashioning: From More to Shakespeare*. Chicago: University of Chicago Press, first 1980, with a New Preface, 2005.

Greenblatt, Stephen. *Cultural Mobility: A Manifesto*. UK & New York: Cambridge University Press, 2010.

Schechner, Richard. Ed. *Performance Studies: An Introduction*. London and New York: Routledge, 2002.

Schwartz, Murray M. "Shakespeare through Contemporary Psychoanalysis." *Representing Shakespeare: New Psychoanalytic Essays*. Eds. Murray M. Schwartz and Coppélia Kahn. Baltimore: The Johns Hopkins University Press, 1980.

Wang, Ban. "Reimagining Political Community: Diaspora, Nation-State, and the Struggle for Recognition." 48:3 (2005), pp.249–271.

CHAPTER 8

Irresistible Seduction and Translocal Labor of Musical Theater in Taiwan: From Translation to Multi-arts

Abstract Musical theater in Taiwan has been importing Broadway musicals to stage various aesthetic styles. Most rely on translation, such as *Kiss Me Nana* by Godot Theatre, translated from *Kiss Me Kate*. Few are faithful presentations in English. Some are opera and film adaptations—*Love Ends in Night Shanghai* (2002) adapted from Alexandre Dumas fils' *La Dame aux Camelias*, *Running Angel* (2005) adapted from the film *Sister Act*, and so on. Some are original—*See the Sun* (2000) on Taiwanese aboriginal ethnicity, and *April Rain* (2007), a Taiwanese musical on Hakka composer Deng Yu-Hsien's love story during Japanese colonialization. Recent trends, *Mulan* (2011) on gender issues, Jolin and Pao's multi-art (pop music and musical) *PK* (2015), and review of Hakka musical *Xiangsi Nostalgia* (2016) are provided.

Keywords Musical theater • Translation • Translocality • Godot Theatre • Multi-arts

INTRODUCTION

This chapter analyzes the dynamics of musicals and their reception in the local context in Asia, and inspects the recent trends from translation and importation toward adaptation and creation in musical theater in Taiwan. From global to local, examining performance as labor and

© The Author(s) 2018
I. H. Tuan, *Translocal Performance in Asian Theatre and Film*,
https://doi.org/10.1007/978-981-10-8609-0_8

labor as performance, musical theater in Taiwan has for some time been importing Broadway musicals for different modes of performing to present various aesthetic styles. Few are faithful performances in English. Exploring musical theater in Taiwan in the theoretical frame of translocality and translation, this chapter focuses on Asian creative local musical, the new performance of the Hakka musical *Xiangsi Nostalgia* (《香絲 相思》 (June 5, 2016, Taipei) produced by Taipei National University of the Arts to stage at the National Theater. I argue that the performance is a high-end collaborative mental and physical labor. No matter what forms or styles, among adaptation and creation works, translation is a significant translocal undertaking in staging musical theater in Taiwan.

Translocality of Musical Theater

Moreover, Asian musical theater translates or adapts Broadway musicals to create its own Asian voice. From English to Chinese, Taiwanese, or Hakka language and culture translocation, since European forms of musical theater in early America in the early eighteenth century, the traditional forms of minstrelsy, vaudeville, burlesque, revue, and comic opera and operetta have been transformed into the Asian modernity through translocal cultural collisions, fusion, interaction, heterogeneous intercultural combination, and innovation.

In cultural mobility and diasporic hybridity, I think that in between tradition and modernity local people have mixed synchronic and diachronic feelings. This is particularly apparent in the lines between here and there, now and then, reality and illusion—and the realistic and the fictional landscapes the audiences see are blurred. The flows of people and information are related to translocality. As Arjun Appadurai claims: "The many displaced, deterritorialized, and transient populations that constitute today's ethnoscapes are engaged in the construction of locality" (1996, p. 199). Examining the relationship between the dimensions of global cultural flows, further refracting these disjunctures are *mediascapes* and *ideoscapes*, "which are closely related landscapes of images" (p. 35). Ideas flow in landscapes and the images of the musicals can spread globally. The ideas within the musicals can be conveyed through translation.

TRANSLATION THEORY

With time and space translation theories have evolved from linguistic validation, interpretation, cultural, word for word versus sense for sense, and so on, to translation criticism, technologies like machine translation, to localization. I'm interested in combining the localization of translation and translocality in terms of the musical theater in Taiwan. Localization of translation covers glocalization, internationalization and localization, language localization, and dub localization. Musical theater, with its drama combined with singing and dance, has less of a language barrier than *Xiqu* and Chinese opera. Comparatively, it is easier to adapt the musicals on universal themes into the local musical productions in Taiwan. In terms of glocalization, with its postcolonial influences from the Dutch, Spain, Japan, Mainland China, and the US, Taiwan prefers to absorb European classics and American Broadway musicals, and go further than mere translation to create its own productions with the addition of local culture and specific flavor.

In my view, there are four kinds of musicals in Taiwan—(1) translation, (2) original creation, (3) adaptation, and (4) authentic faithful presentation of the foreign language original. I will analyze each of the musical types in Taiwan and Hong Kong by using related examples.

TRANSLOCAL LABOR OF TRANSLATION

First of all, translation of musicals from English or other foreign language into Mandarin Chinese in Taiwan. Appadurai's translocal concept is applied to the labor of translation in musical theater from one place to the other, from one language to the other, considering different cultures, national identity, and social background, the efforts of translations are understandable. For example, Shakespeare's play *The Taming of the Shrew* is transformed into the musical *Kiss Me Kate*. Then, via translocal adaptation, the English musical *Kiss Me Kate* is translated with time and space difference into the Chinese musical *Kiss Me Nana*.

Most musicals staged in Taiwan rely on translation, with the majority being translated from English to Chinese. For instance, *Kiss Me Nana* (premiered 1997, restaged 1999) (Fig. 8.1)—produced by the Godot Theatre, with script adaptation and lyrics by Chen Le-Jung (陳樂融) and music composition by the talented tenor singer Tom Chang (張雨生, 1966–1997)—was translated from the Broadway musical *Kiss Me Kate* (1948), music and lyrics by Cole Porter.

Fig. 8.1 *Kiss Me Nana*. New Millennium Version (1999–2000). (Courtesy of Godot Theatre)

Although there are some differences between *Kiss Me Kate* and *Kiss Me Nana*, as Steven Suskin in *Broadway Yearbook 1999–2000* comments, *Kiss Me Kate* is "All in all, capital entertainment" (2001, p. 85). I also think *Kiss Me Nana* provides audiences with capital entertainment.

Not just in Taiwan, but most musicals across Asia are translated from English into Chinese. For example, *Rent* (1996 official opening), with music and lyrics by Jonathan Larson and loosely based on Giacomo Puccini's opera *La Bohème*, was translated from English into Chinese and performed in Cantonese to become the Chinese version of *Rent* 《吉屋出租》 (premiered 2006) in Hong Kong. The role of Mimi was played by the famous female singer Karen Mok (莫文蔚), who was the first female popular singer to appear in a Broadway musical in Asia. This production also toured in Taiwan and Beijing.

RECEPTION

Chunminmou's performance review in Taipei claimed that Karen Mok who played the role of Mimi—a sexy pole dancer who has AIDS and a drug problem—danced adequately and sang well enough, even tried hard, but still cannot perform as well as the Broadway musical singers in this rock musical. Nevertheless, he feels that at least Mok did not ruin this musical.

ASIAN ORIGINAL CREATIONS

From *Kiss Me Kate* to *Kiss Me Nana*, and the Chinese version of *Rent*, the musical theater in Asia has demonstrated its ability to stage not just the Broadway musicals in English, but also in Asian languages (such as Cantonese, Mandarin, Taiwanese, Taiwanese aboriginal, Japanese, and Hakka). Some of them are original and innovative local Asian inventions; for instance, *Snow Wolf Lake* (1997) by the well-known popular Hong Kong singer Jacky H. Cheung (張學友), *See the Sun* (2000) on the Taiwanese aboriginal ethnicity issue, and the first Taiwanese musical *April Rain* (2007).

PLOT, RECEPTION, IMPACT

Snow Wolf Lake (in Cantonese, premiered 1997; in Mandarin, restaged 2004–2007) is the first well known original modern musical in Hong Kong. Jacky H. Cheung, the famous popular singer, working as artistic director and male lead, contributed a lot to making this musical artistic and successful. *Snow Wolf Lake* is about the love story between Gardener Hu Wolf and the rich lady whose family he works for, Peace Snow. It is based on the novel *The Wolf's Heart* written by Chung Wei-Min. There are two acts in the performance, which lasts three hours. In the end of the tragedy, Hu embraces Snow's dead body and they sink into the lake together leaving the audience sad.

The reception of *Snow Wolf Lake* has been great. This musical has been a huge box-office success. It is a big production, with a cast and crew of more than 300 people (for the continuous forty-two performances in Hong Kong in 1997) and audience numbers estimated to be more than 300,000. The music album of *Snow Wolf Lake* won the double Platinum Award in 1997. The theme song "Ageless Legend" was the best-seller that year.

The musical went on to successfully tour in Singapore, where it achieved great acclaim and broke the record for the number of performances staged and audience numbers. The Mandarin version of this musical was staged in 2004–2007 across Asia, in Beijing, Taipei, other cities in China, Singapore, and Malaysia, receiving excellent reviews and box-office sell outs. The success of *Snow Wolf Lake* (which is ingenuous in its combination popular music with operetta) has had a big impact on Chinese musicals in Asia. Many pop singers regard the musical as the other path to follow for their careers. Furthermore, with pop singers starring in musicals, more and more people have become interested in going to theater to enjoy the shows. *Snow Wolf Lake*, a big and excellent production, is still the most popular original Chinese musical so far.

I think the contributing factors to the success of this musical include having the famous pop singer Jacky H. Cheung as the male lead, nice songs, a sad and touching tragic love story, the miracle of the lovers coming back together to the "time wound" to see the past to try to heal it, the spectacular stage design, the sheer size of the production, and the new, brave spirit of creating the first original Chinese musical in Asia (Fig. 8.2).

Fig. 8.2 The Taiwanese aborigine young man sings of his despair and hope in the musical *See the Sun*. (Courtesy of Godot Theatre)

Theme, Reception, Comments

In Taiwan, *See the Sun* is the first original musical script performed by the Godot Theatre. The theme is Taiwanese aborigines' survival in the modern urban city of Taipei. The story follows a Taiwanese aborigine brother and sister through their tough lives in the modern society of capitalism. They cannot make a living on the mountains as their aborigine ancestors did before. They have to come to the metropolitan city to try to earn their bread, despite being faced with exploitation and low wages. This musical also deals with the stereotypes and problems of the Taiwanese aborigines, such as drinking, prostitutes, unfair education chances, and mistreatment due to prejudice. It is original in its addition of Taiwanese aborigines' ritual dance, myth, and singing, making it a unique local musical (Fig. 8.2).

April Rain 《四月望雨》 (2007), the first acclaimed Taiwanese musical, is about the love story of the Hakka composer Deng Yu-Hsien (鄧雨賢, 1906–1944), who rid himself of the burden of tradition to dedicate himself to the modern "dance era" during Japanese colonialization. This original musical creates brand new scores and lyrics using Deng's most famous four songs—"Rainy Night Flower" (《雨夜花》), "Spring Breeze" (or "Whispering Hope" 《望春風》), "Moon Night Sorrow" (《月夜愁》), and "Four Seasons Red" (《四季紅》). The four songs symbolize joy, sorrow, hope, and annihilation, which reflect society and milieu under Japanese colonialization in Taiwan at that time.

This original Taiwanese musical is performed mainly in Taiwanese, imbued with Mandarin and Hakka language, and a little Japanese. Deng was passionate about creating change for music in Taiwan during Japan's colonialization and the cruel World War I. Deng was renowned as the "father of Taiwanese ballads."

This Taiwanese musical, *April Rain*, was sponsored by Younglin Foundation and staged by All Music Theater. The artistic team is full of professionals, including artistic director and original script playwright Yang Chung-Heng, composer (Jan Tien-Hao), Taiwanese lyrics and dramaturge by Wang Yu-Hui, Hakka lyrics by Chung Yung-Feng. Direction and script adaptation is by Yang Shih-Ping.

This original Taiwanese musical has an abstract implicit emergent Taiwan cultural atmosphere, as Pei-Hsin comments: [it] presents Taiwanese people's characteristic of "the roses which cannot be pressed flat." Even through tremendous torture, we can still be reborn after spring rain. This musical depicts the story of dream, hope, annihilation, and rebirth. It intends to

Fig. 8.3 Composer Deng Yu-Hsien and the singer's love story in *April Rain*. (Courtesy of All Music Theater)

express the strong spirit of Taiwanese people, soft yet resilient, concerned with the world and love. *April Rain* expects that Taiwan, Formosa, beautiful island, can eventually become a peaceful and joyous island. (2011).

In 2007, immediately after the first Hakka musical *My Daughter's Wedding*, *April Rain* received compliments from the critics and applause from local Taiwanese audiences. Appealing to the island's national identity, the Taiwanese musical *April Rain* has great good box-office success (Fig. 8.3).

The creative Chinese musical script for *Mulan* received first prize in the *Fucheng* (Tainan City) Literature Awards. Directed by Lu Bo-Sen, playwright and actor Pao-Chang Tsai's provocative musical was produced by Tainan Jen Theatre. *Mulan* was selected to be staged in 2009 to celebrate the tenth anniversary of the establishment of the Department of Drama at National Taiwan University. This creative and provocative musical on gender issues was restaged at the National Theater in 2011.

The musical *Mulan* challenges gender and relationship stereotypes. The plot becomes complex when the male army generals are confused as to whether they have fallen in love with the man or the woman. The story also adds some contemporary social situations, such as introducing the element of the eldest daughter being pregnant outside of marriage, which means she cannot take her elderly father's place in the army. The youngest son is homosexual and this might cause him a lot of trouble if he were to serve in his father's place in the army. The creative additions of the funny plots, in superb mise-en-scène, modern singing, and dance make this original *Mulan* special. (Fig. 8.4).

Fig. 8.4 The musical *Mulan* was inspired by and adapted from the animated film. (Courtesy of Director Lu Poshen, Tainan Jen Theatre, and Photographer Chen, Yu-Wei)

ADAPTATION

Thirdly, some musicals are (major or minor) opera and film adaptations; for instance, *Love Ends in Night Shanghai* (2002, Taipei) adapted from Alexandre Dumas fils' novel *La Dame aux Camelias*, *Running Angel* (2005) adapted from the film *Sister Act* (1992), and *My Daughter's Wedding* (2007) adapted from Shakespeare's *The Taming of the Shrew*.

The adaptation *Love Ends in Night Shanghai* changes the setting from Paris in France to Shanghai in China in the second decade of the early twentieth century. In the adaptation, the story is condensed to be about the transition year in which Courtesan Bai Yu-wei enjoyed life, fell in love, and went from living a luxurious life to a plain one. She is sacrificed for love. Eventually, she was so depressed that she passed away. Tsai Chin, the famous folk singer, playing the role of Courtesan Bai, sings well in her deep Alto voice.

Another example of adaptation is *Hello Dolly!* According to Mu Yu, director and choreography Gower Champion has done "an excellent piece of work in *Hello Dolly!* (1964) which won him a decisive success" (2012, p. 172). This musical is about the matchmaker Dolly's love story. The Chinese version *Hello, Dolly!* (《我愛紅娘》) (2010, Taipei), adapted from the Broadway musical, is directed by Liang Chi-Ming's Godot Theatre and performed in Manadrin.

Famous TV hostess Bai Bin-Bin stars as Dolly. Musician and lyricist Chen Kuo-Hwang mixes Japanese pop songs, American jazz dance, and a live big band, in collaboration with Ju Tzong-Ching's Percussion Group. The dance style is a combination of samba, salsa, modern ballet, rectified Indian dance, tango, and so on. This musical combines the multi-art of theatrical art and TV talk show.

Authentic Faithful Presentation of the Foreign Language

Last but not least, some musicals faithful "authentic" presentations in French or English, staged in Taipei. For instance, *Notre Dame de Paris* (《鐘樓怪人》) is adapted from Victor Hugo's novel and sung in French (premiered in Taipei 2005, restaged in Taipei 2013, April 2015, male lead Matt Laurent). Others include *Romeo et Juliet* (2016 Taipei), *Le Petit Prince* (《小王子》) (Asia tour 2007, 2016, Taipei), and *French Musical GALA Concert* (2016 Taipei).

European forms have influenced musical theater in Taiwan as well as in some other countries in Asia. European forms (such as the ballad opera, comic opera, pasticcio, minstrelsy, vaudeville, burlesque, revue, operetta) dominated musical in early colonial America. According to Richard Kislan in *The Musical: A Look at the American Musical Theater*: "Although importation declined when native talent emerged, the earliest work of the American artists was never less than European in form, style, and spirit" (1995, p. 11). Similarly, through importation of European musicals, Taiwan has learned to develop the various forms of musical theater and cultivate the talent to create original musicals based on the local culture.

Inviting famous musicals from France to perform at the Taipei Arena is very lucrative for the creative industry. It goes without saying that those authentic musicals from Europe, Canada, and the US are very popular in Taiwan. And these musicals inspire the emergence of native talent to produce innovative cross-boundary multi-arts in Taiwan.

MULTI-ART

Jolin and Pao's *PK* (2015) is a collaboration between pop music and the theater. Jolin Tsai is a popular singer who has received many music prizes, including the Golden Melody Award (2007), and held many successful concerts, including at the Taipei Arena. Pao-Chang Tsai, a young theater director, playwright, and actor in his late thirties, is gradually emerging from the Experimental Little Theater to the Tainan Jen Theatre to the musical theater in Taiwan. This cross boundary collaboration is initiated and performed at the National Theater in Taipei. The idea is that Jolin Tsai taught the male director and actor Pao-Chang Tsai how to dance in high-heeled shoes and sing the song "Play我呸." In return, Pao-Chang Tsai taught the singer Jolin Tsai how to play the role of Juliet in Shakespeare's *Romeo and Juliet* in order to perform the famous monologue in the balcony scene.

> JULIET.
> O Romeo, Romeo! wherefore art thou Romeo?
> Deny thy father and refuse thy name;
> Or, if thou wilt not, be but sworn my love,
> And I'll no longer be a Capulet.
> (Skip Romeo's Aside line.)
> 'Tis but thy name that is my enemy;
> Thou art thyself, though not a Montague.
> What's Montague? it is nor hand, nor foot,
> Nor arm, nor face, nor any other part
> Belonging to a man. O, be some other name!
> What's in a name? that which we call a rose
> By any other name would smell as sweet;
> So Romeo would, were he not Romeo call'd,
> Retain that dear perfection which he owes
> Without that title. Romeo, doff thy name,
> And for that name which is no part of thee
> Take all myself.
> (Act 2, Scene 2)

After translation, Tsai performed this monologue in Mandarin. The result is that both of them recognize the efforts and progress of each other. Pao-Chang Tsai, wearing a pair of red super high-heeled shoes, is camp, flamboyant, conceited, and arrogant, shakes his hips sexily while singing the alluring pop song. Jolin Tsai is in her thirties and has no prior

Fig. 8.5 Jolin Tsai and Pao-Chang Tsai's *PK* (2015). (Courtesy of National Theatre)

acting experience. She is quite shy and charming as she portrays the young teenager Juliet pining for love. Although not exactly a musical, Jolin Tsai and Pao-Chang Tsai's *PK* work is a new multi-art collaboration of music, dance, and drama in the modern pop form (Fig. 8.5).

Hakka Musical "*Xiangsi Nostalgia*"

Nine years after the first Hakka musical, a second, *Xiangsi* (Lovesickness) *Nostalgia* (2016) was staged in Taiwan. (Fig. 8.6). As already discussed, *My Daughter's Wedding* (2007), an adaptation of Shakespeare's *Taming of the Shrew*, was the first Hakka musical. Both were produced by Taipei National University of the Arts and sponsored by Hakka Affairs Council. *Xiangsi Nostalgia* is different in that the script by playwright Lin Chien-Hua is taken from a Taiwanese short story, "Tung Flowers," written by local Hakka author Kung Wan-Tsao (龔萬灶). Issues of ethnicity, love, and class are examined through lovers' misunderstandings set largely in the much simpler 1930s period. The woodcutter Master Hwang's first apprentice, Lee Mu-shen (李木生) (played by Hsu Hao-Hsiang), loves a poetic Hakka girl, Liu Yu-chuan (滿妹, Manmei, "Miss Satisfied or Full"; played by Liu TingFang), whose family (彭城堂) lives on Tai number 3 freeway (Fig. 8.7).

IRRESISTIBLE SEDUCTION AND TRANSLOCAL LABOR OF MUSICAL... 117

Fig. 8.6 The cast in the Hakka musical "*Xiangsi Nostalgia*" (《香絲 相思》) (2016, Taipei). (Courtesy of Hakka Affairs Council)

Fig. 8.7 The lovers in the Hakka musical "*Xiangsi Nostalgia*" (《香絲 相思》) (2016, Taipei). (Courtesy of Hakka Affairs Council)

Xiangsi Nostalgia emphasizes Hakka music and song rather than dance or spectacle, contrasting with the earlier Hakka musical and making up for the previous musical's auditory weakness. *Xiqu* (戲曲) director Lee Hsiao Ping (李小平) received the National Literature and Arts Award (2011) and is noted for his direction of the Guoguang Opera Company (國光劇團), which has staged several productions mixing traditional Chinese Peking opera and modern theater, such as *Meng Xiaodong, Cleopatra and Her Crowns*. Here he represented Hakka women's longing for love in the 1930s. Miss Full loves Lee Mushen, yet misunderstandings and a mutual love that is never clearly discussed block their implicit love. Miss Full is left longing and full of sorrow, thinking herself abandoned after Lee's death in an accident. She dies having never discovered the truth.

The play involves six scenes. Pingmei (Flat Girl, 平妹; played by Chien Yu-Lun), Liu's adopted daughter, narrates and commemorates Manmei, Liu's daughter, with whom she has a good relationship. Manmei is sensitive and pretty, and has memorized many Chinese poems, yet has a crippled leg. Pingmei, born to a poor family, has been adopted by the Liu family as a child to be a household helper and, when she grows up, to marry Liu's son in the tradition of a child bride (童養媳, *tung yang hsi*). One rainy day, the woodcutter Master Hwang and his young apprentices, including Lee Mu-shen (李木生, literally "Wood Birth"), take shelter at Liu's house.

There is no real climax in this lyrical Hakka musical, making the performance rhythm rather slow and flat, but giving emphasis to the Hakka singing. Only at the beginning of the final scene is there a revelation. In contrast to scene 5, in which Manmei with sorrow laments that she must wait for Lee, in the final scene 6 we learn that many years have passed and Pingmei's teenager daughter accompanies the Liu family to Manmei's burial place for the tomb-sweeping festival. Suddenly we realize that Manmei died of sorrow. At first the viewer assumes Lee abandoned her. However, a stranger, who is actually Lee's nephew, appears, and the audience members learn Lee died in an accident long before Manmei's death. Underneath Lee's pillow, there was always the cherished poetry book that Manmei had lent him. When Manmei's aged mother brings the book to Manmei's tomb, saying, "Alas! Manmei, he does *not* forget you!" the audience members, who included the current Taiwanese president as well as myself, were deeply touched, and many were moved to tears. The powerful ending of the performance left a feeling of high artistic achievement.

An orchestra and chorus accompanied the live performance at the National Theater with Hwang Pei-Shu (黃珮舒), a strong Hakka singer, playing Yu-Niang (羽娘, Lady of Feathers, the symbol of the white crane = fate). With many Hakka images of white tung flowers, flowery clothes, and blue shirts, in *Xiangsi Nostalgia* artistic director Wu Jung-Shun (吳榮順) tried to "let the audience members see, through this performance, the spirit of Hakka humanity, feelings and dialogue under Acacia, the Xiangsi" (相思, "I Miss You") trees (= the same pronunciation of 香絲 in Hakka language). The poetics celebrated Hakka ancestors' lesson of "cultivating on sunny days and reading on raining days" (晴耕雨讀) (*Xiangsi Nostalgia* 2016, p. 4).

Manmei, whose name in Chinese characters (滿妹) means "satisfied or full girl," died of heartbreak without discovering that she was loved in return. Her name is ironic since she dies young and full of regret. The surprise reversal in the final scene saves this nostalgic Hakka musical. However, the plot did not seem reasonable. Lee's master would have told Manmei's father that the young man had died in the accident, allowing Manmei to know he did not desert her. Lee's nephew's sudden revelation, however, left viewers with a strong emotional impression.

There were two weddings in *My Daughter's Wedding*, while *Xiangsi Nostalgia* had only one wedding for the living, working against the standard musical model of a happy ending. Lee, however, designed the closing scene to allow Manmei's family and the young nephew to circle on the forestage (choreography by Tung I-Fen) beneath Manmei's tomb in a slow-motion dance with music to comfort the souls of the dead. As director, he also added the symbolic wedding for the dead: Manmei and Lee Mu-shen appeared wearing traditional red bridal costumes (designed by Chen Wan-Li and Chen Chia-Min) and holding the red long ribbons representing union. The effective stage design was done by Wang Shih-Hsin, with lighting by Chien Li-Ren. The couple bowed beneath a red arch. Holding a wedding for the dead, which is still done among Hakka today, is a traditional custom called sacred marriage (冥婚). In this scene the atmosphere was transformed into a ritual uniting the couple in heaven.

In *My Daughter's Wedding*, as I wrote in a previous performance review (Tuan 2011), the authors contemporized and localized the work, emphasizing dance and spectacle via "local color," but the troupe was reprimanded for neglecting Hakka song. *Xiangsi Xiangsi Nostalgia*, by contrast, emphasized dialogue, singing with correct Hakka pronunciation. The musicians and the chorus in the orchestra pit added to the effect (Fig. 8.8).

Fig. 8.8 Pingmei (平妹 Flat Girl)'s wedding in the Hakka Musical *Xiangsi Nostalgia* (2016, Taipei). (Courtesy of Hakka Affairs Council)

This performance was lyrical rather than theatrical, with a much higher standard of Hakka songs, composed by Yen Ming-Hsiu, who included Hakka traditional mountain songs, small tunes (滿妹), and *Pingban* (平板) to meet the cultural policy of the Hakka Affairs Council. Although we had to wait nine years for this second Hakka musical, perhaps we can look forward to a third soon: with Tsai Yin-Wen's election as Taiwan's first female president and a Hakka ethnic sworn into office on 20 May 20, 2016, and her Democratic People Party (DPP)'s ruling the country, we look forward to her fulfilling her promise of supporting Hakka culture and upholding the DPP's national policy of localization and internationalization.

Musical theater in Taiwan has developed from translating or importing Western musicals to creating local musicals. The legacy of the musical lives on across Europe, America, and now Asia: Taiwan is in the process defining the nature of the Taiwanese musical.

Critics' and Scholars' Comments

In the program for *Xiangsi Nostalgia* TNUA President Yang Chi-wen points out the "lovesickness; that, even across great distance, they miss each other continually. According to Yang:

> Missing someone, a deep concern, is the most difficult obstacle for human beings to get over. Puzzled by feeling, tortured by feeling, they think of love, loss of love, and dream for love. (2016, p. 3)

The female protagonist Manmei died of missing the man she loved without knowing that she was loved in return. As mentioned in the previous section, her name Manmei, which in Chinese characters (滿妹) means "Satisfied Girl" or "Full Girl", is actually ironic because she is not satisfied at all. Instead, she is crippled, does not live her life to the full, and dies young, full of regret.

> Love comes at a cost, as the ancient Chinese poet Liu Yung's poem suggests:
> The dress takes to loosen gradually and I am more and more emaciated,
> No regretful plying at all, I am rather for her/him only distressed as I did.

Even a king would give up his kingdom for true love
With regard to the script, I think that the plot arrangement is flawed. It is not reasonable for Lee Mu-shen's master not tell Manmei's father that the male protagonist had died in an accident. If he had done, Manmei would know of his death and that she had not been deserted by him without any news or letters. Before the intermission, the performance was flat and slow without any major action. After intermission, however, when the stranger (Lee Mu-shen's young nephew) appears to reveal the truth, the sudden realization and surprise altered the audience's reaction to the whole performance from so-so to good.

Comparison of the Two Hakka Musicals

In a comparison of the two Hakka musicals, with regard to the labor of translating and adapting the script, the first Hakka Musical, *My Daughter's Wedding*,

> cut Shakespeare's prologue and five scenes, simplifying the play to quicken the pace of the story as the narrative mixed up time and space. ... The deconstruction of Shakespeare's frame story and removal of the Elizabethan

concept of the patriarchal power allowed for a reinterpretation of gender roles. Modern music and professional dance numbers attracted applause. References to Internet cafés, online games, motorcycle machismo, and contemporary military culture made the production up to date, while traditional Hakka elements is set, clothing, female advisement, and wedding customs increased local flavor. The mixture reflected contemporary life and made the work distinctly Taiwanese. (Tuan 2011, pp. 576–577)

Even though this recent second Hakka musical *Xiangsi Nostalgia* lacks the excellent dance and the spectacle of the first Hakka Musical *My Daughter's Wedding*, *Xiangsi Nostalgia* avoids the negative comments the first Hakka musical got. For example, *Xiangsi Nostalgia* has merits in not using too many artificial cultural constructed Hakka images. And the second Hakka musical includes more dialogues, conversations, monologues, and singing in correct and pure Hakka pronunciation. The cast also collaborates well with the live orchestra and the choir who sing Hakka songs underneath the orchestra pit.

Conclusion

The legacy of the musical is apparent throughout Europe, America, and Asia. As David A. Crespy points out, "the example of 1960s pioneers drove theater across America to this day. Off-off-Broadway stages are found thousands of miles from New York—in Seattle, Minneapolis, Austin, Chicago, Los Angeles—wherever there are artists hungry to produce fresh work" (2003, p. 13). Travelling across landscapes, the musical theater in Taiwan has carved a path from translocal labor of translation, in the process of adaptation and authenticity, to original multi-art creations.

As Steven Suskin believes, "Color is and should be inconsequential" (2001, p. 86). There is no race problem in Taiwan, but the musical theater in Taiwan reflects the concerns and issues of class, gender, and ethnicity. From the examples and the case study in this chapter, we can see that musical theater in Taiwan has transformed from translation to multi-arts with local cultural characteristics. As high-end art produced through collaborative mental and physical musical theater in Taiwan has developed from translating, importing Broadway musicals, and inviting European musicals in French to perform in Taiwan to creating her own local musicals.

Even though nothing lasts forever, with time and translocal space, no matter whether we are speaking in Chinese, Taiwanese, Hakka, Japanese, or English, translation labor, multi-arts, and various aesthetic performing styles have bloomed into full beautiful flowers in the musical theater of Taiwan.

BIBLIOGRAPHY

Appadurai, Arjun. 1996. *Modernity at Large: Cultural Dimensions of Globalization.* Minneapolis and London: University of Minnesota Press.
Crespy, A. David. 2003. *Off-Off Broadway Explosion.* Foreword by Edward Albee. New York: Back Stage Books.
Kislan, Richard. 1995. *The Musical: A Look at the American Musical Theater.* New York and London: Applause.
Suskin, Steven. 2001. *Broadway Yearbook 1999–2000.* Oxford and New York: Oxford University Press.
Tuan, Iris Hsin-chun. 2011. "My Daughter's Wedding." *Asian Theatre Journal.* Vol. 28. Num. 2: 573–577.
Yu, Mu. 2012. *Broadway Musical.* (《百老匯音樂劇》). Taipei: Da-Di Press.
Program of Xiangsi Nostalgia, Hakka Musical. 2016. Sponsored by Hakka Affairs Council. Produced by Taipei National University of the Arts.
Hakka TV advertisement. https://www.youtube.com/watch?v=C4gHcH4exxY. Retrieved on June 8, 2016.
Chunminmou. 2006. "Review of Rent in Taipei Version." (〈劇評:吉屋出租台北版〉) http://blog.udn.com/chunminmau/347431. Retrieved on June 17, 2016.
Pei-Hsin (培心). 2011. "The Importance of *April Rain* in the History of the Musical in Taiwan." (〈《四月望雨》之於台灣歷史在音樂劇表現的重要性〉) http://artmagazine.com.tw/ArtCritic/article825.html. Retrieved on June 17, 2016. Performance film clips
"Karen Mok—The first female artist plays the Broadway Musical *Rent*." https://www.youtube.com/watch?v=l57sVhzJXWQ. Retrieved on June 8, 2016.
Jolin and Pao's *PK* (2015) between the pop music and the musical. https://www.youtube.com/watch?v=M4jqk2LFWvA; https://www.youtube.com/watch?v=NNFydaipe3k Retrieved on June 8, 2016.
The Hakka musical "*Xiangsi Nostalgia*" (《香絲 相思》) (2016) Hakka TV advertisement. https://www.youtube.com/watch?v=C4gHcH4exxY Retrieved on June 8, 2016.
Yang, Chi-wen. Xiangsi Nostalgia. 2016 [Program.] Sponsored by Hakka Affairs Council and produced by Taipei National University of the Arts.

CHAPTER 9

Spectacle, Adaptation, and Sexuality in Chinese Musicals

Abstract The musical, with singing and dance, can be presented through visual spectacle, strengthening plot, character, thought, diction, and music to tell the story better. The musical *Mountains and Seas* (premiered 2013, restage May 2017, Taipei) is directed by Liang, Chi-Ming. The script is adapted from the play written by the 2000 Nobel Prize winner Gao Xing-Jian (1940–). Documenting the history of the development of Chinese musical in China and Taiwan and exploring the motifs of hypermedia, hypertext, and literary studies, I argue that the issues of love, sexuality, and war aided by visual spectacle are more fascinating to watch and match present day audience's tastes in a post-Aristotle multimedia high-technology era.

Keywords Spectacle • Adaptation • Sexuality • *Kiss Me Nana*
• *Mountains and Seas*

INTRODUCTION: THE EXCHANGE OF SPECTACLE
IN MUSICAL THEATER

The transfer of spectacle visual elements that represent wars and sexuality translocally crosses cultures and history to the contemporary performance by adaptation in Chinese musicals. This chapter explores how the spectacle supports and strengthens plot, character, thought, diction, and music in musical theater. Examples include: the spectacular chandelier in the Baroque style opéra de Paris and the gondola scene in the Phantom's home in the cellars of the Opera House in *Phantom of the Opera* in the nineteenth century; the helicopter in *Miss Saigon* in the setting of the 1970s during the Vietnam War; the big ship scene in *Les Misérables* with the novel background of beginning in 1815 and culminating in the 1832 June Rebellion in Paris. These devices to transport the historic events onto the contemporary global performance stages. But, how does the visual spectacle help the poetic elements to tell the story and portray the characters and their actions better in the Chinese musical?

Las Vegas is a good venue for spectacle—the last element in Aristotle's *Poetics*. Yet spectacle merely attracts audiences' eyes, especially in the contemporary age of media. The slogan may claim that "What happens in Vegas, stays in Vegas," but Vegas actually has a great impact on theatrical performances worldwide. That is why, despite being an isolated artificial city in the desert, still millions of tourists, especially Asians, swarm into Las Vegas every year. Imitations of Vegas are also found in Macaw and Dubai, and perhaps in adult fantasy dreamlands everywhere. Thus, visual spectacle can be viewed as a cultural exchange through musical theater and dance across geography and history to the contemporary world.

Spectacle, Adaptation, and Sexuality in Chinese Adaptation

This chapter explores the issues of spectacle, adaptation, and sexuality in the Chinese musicals produced by China, with a focus on Taiwan. As mentioned, spectacle supports and strengthens plot, character, thought, diction, and music in musical theater to tell the story (either original or adaptation) better. Both China and Taiwan have learned from the Western musicals to develop their own Chinese musicals, such as the new Chinese original musical *Queen of Coquetry* (November 12, 2016, Taipei), produced by Shanghai Spoken Drama Art Center and staged in Taipei. Not only producing original works but also doing their own adaptations, Taiwan's well-known Godot Theatre's restaging of *Kiss Me Nana* (premiered 1997, 1999, December 2016, Taipei), adapted from the Broadway Musical *Kiss Me Kate*, and other musicals focus on the issues of class, love, sexuality, and spectacle.

Applying the theories to practice, first I describe the history and development of the musical in China and Taiwan, then I analyze and comment on the case study, before drawing the conclusion. In methodology and approach, I use the theory of inter-media, technology, digital historiography, performance, real experience of watching the performance in Taipei, an interview of the director in my case study, and the research literature.

THEORIES

To legitimate the importance of spectacle, in theory, I refer to books and journal papers concerning inter-media, technology, and digital historiography to explore the theme of spectacle in performance. In terms of performance, digital technologies, and history, Sarah Bay-Cheng's paper "Digital Historiography and Performance" in *Theatre Journal* uses German artist Thomas Tayrle's *iPhone Meets Caravaggio*, a 2015 digital image, to speak to "a contemporary phenomenon of digital technologies, mass communication, and history" (2016, p. 509). As Bay-Cheng indicates, it is not just the conferences such as IFTR, ASTR, and ATHE organizing groups on digital humanities, giving awards on digital scholarship, and so on. I also notice that *Theatre Journal*, *Theatre Topics*, and *Contemporary Theatre Review* have either sections on digital methodologies or online addendum in recent issues on theater and performance studies (2016, p. 510). What are digital technologies and digital scholarship? Bay-Cheng refers to "digital historiography and performance" as an area of study that "occupies overlapping domains among digital technologies (computers, video recorders, and mobile media), new computational methodologies (for example, so called big-data analyses, web-scraping, and online media miming), history, and a diverse range of performance practices, including theater, performance art, and dance" (2016, p. 513).

As the history is rewritten on interfaces such as mobile phones, the distinction between fiction and reality is blurred. I think that the intertextuality is complex among the paper documents and the performance becomes multi-layered, floating between media. So, we might heed Aristotle's theory in *Poetics* (c. 335 BCE) that spectacle—that is, "Everything that is seen or heard on stage," including, "(a)ctors, sets, costumes, lights and sound"[1]—should not be over-estimated. Spectacle is the last element in Aristotle's six elements—(1) plot, (2) character, (3) theme, (4) rhythm, (5) language, and (6) spectacle—because, as he claims,

---

[1] 6 Aristotelian Elements of A Play, retrieved from https://www.bellevuecollege.edu/artshum/materials/drama/Hoffman/101SIXARISTOAPLAYspr03.asp. June 27, 2017.

a tragedy does not need to be performed to have an impact on the audience, it can just as easily be read as a text.

Richard Wagner attests that "total theater" is an integration of all elements in theater, including spectacle. In terms of spectacle and digital technologies, as Randall Packer points out, "Richard Wagner's ideas and work constitute a powerful means for understanding the subsequent emergence of interdisciplinary forms: from the spectacles of nineteenth-century opera to the birth of film in the early twentieth century, to the electronic art, video, happenings, and theater of mixed-means of the 1960s, and to the interactive forms of digital multimedia that now play out on the display of the personal computer" (2011, p. 156). Nowadays in our digital e-era, all the elements of drama, lyrics, music, dance, stage action, scenery, props, lighting, and stage design can be integrated into the artistic whole total theater via media and digital technologies to amplify the audio and visual effects.

Not facetiously, I think spectacle can really help the audience to see the interweaving of elements and understand the literary form, as George Landow and Paul Delany describe, as "intertextualities" (2001, p. 226). Hypertext, as the example of reading a lot of footnotes back and forth in James Joyce's *Ulysees*, indicated by Landow and Delany, refers to "almost exclusively to computerized hypertext programs, and to the textual structures that can be composed with their aid" (2001, p. 227). Spectacle can make the literary form vivid in adaptation to present the theme of sexuality via hypermedia. Landow and Delany point out that:

> Hypermedia takes us even closer to the complex interrelatedness of everyday consciousness; it extends hypertext by re-integrating our visual and auditory faculties into textual experience, linking graphic images, sound and video to verbal signs. Hypermedia seeks to approximate the way our waking minds always make a synthesis of information received from all five senses. Integrating or (re-integrating) touch, taste and smell seems the inevitable consummation of the hypermedia concept. (2001, p. 231)

In my view, our five senses, especially the audio and visual, can be more sensitive to exploring the meaning of the literary form and the hypertext in order to understand the inter-textuality if aided by spectacle and hypermedia. This helps the audience members to comprehend the multiple layers of meaning in the Chinese musical, especially the adaptation from the Western musical. Let's now trace back the history and development of the musical in China and Taiwan.

HISTORY AND DEVELOPMENT OF THE MUSICAL IN CHINA, TAIWAN, AND HONG KONG

Chinese traditional music has a five-thousand-year tradition, however, it also has been influenced by Western music. As Fang Kun et al claimed in a discussion about the Second Oriental Music Festival at Durham, England from August 9–18, 1979: "Traditional Chinese music is slow, so where does such violent and complicated music as *Ambush on all Sides* come from? ... Obviously they have been influenced by Western music;" (1981, p. 3). It goes without saying that in the globalization of the twentieth-first century, alongside Disney films and TV musicals, Western musicals—such as the European English and French musicals in the West End in London and Broadway musicals in New York—have a huge impact on Chinese musicals.

On August 9–10, 1987, the importation of *The Music Man* and *The Fantasticks* into China started the formal influence of the Broadway musical on China (Chiu 2008, p. 59). China learns from Broadway musical, not only the musical drama style, but also the marketing methods for repertory theater and touring performances in different cities. By 2007, China had imported several Broadway musicals, including *The Sound of Music, My Fair Lady, Phantom of the Opera, Les Misérables, Cats*, and *Mama Mia!*, to name just a few.

Disney's High School Musical: Localized and Internationalized

Western musical influence on China doesn't come just from the importation of the mega musicals (e.g., *Phantom of the Opera, Miss Saigon, Les Misérables, Cats*, etc.) from England and the US. Disney also grabs part of the big cake in the extensive wide ranging market in China. According to Katalin Lustyik in the journal paper "Disney's High School Musical: Music makes the world go 'round'," "With the growing consumer power of teens, tweens and even younger children, this niche group represents a 'powerful force in popular music' today" (Lustyik 2012, p. 417). Disney maximizes this power by using franchises, the most successful global commercial strategy, to distribute *Disney's High School Musical* in multimedia, to target the above age group.

Quintessentially they do this by using what Lustyik calls "the three specific types of customization of the High School Musical trilogy: (1) customization of songs and the soundtrack(s); (2) customization of national and regional promotional and marketing campaigns that incorporated dance competitions; and (3) the customization of the musical itself that represents the most in-depth adaptation of media content" (2013, pp. 244–245). In so doing, Disney's fairy tale themes of dreams come true, music, and dance can be customized for different media, and. Disney spreads its astounding power in China and across the world. Lustyik notices that:

> The management team of Disney Asia, the regional headquarters which focus on Southeast Asia, decided to replicate the dance group competition Disney's High School Musical 247 in selected countries, including Malaysia, Singapore and Taiwan in 2007. The following year, the regional Disney team expanded the competition and turned it into an inter-country contest enlisting Indonesia, Korea, Papua New Guinea, Vietnam and others nations. Children from over a dozen countries between the ages of 10 and 17 were encouraged to form dance groups to participate. The performances that made it into the finals were shown on Disney Channels throughout the region, and the teams travelled to Disneyland Hong Kong to dance in front of a live audience. The success of the My School Rocks! in India and the inter-country dance competitions that took part in Southeast Asia is based on the familiarity and popularity of the Bollywood-film format in the region and its proximity to the High School Musical. Such widespread success, however, could not have been achieved without the expanding Disney infrastructure in the region: the television channels and the websites that provide a 24-hour connection with fans. Customizing the soundtracks and part of the promotional campaign through these dance competitions were very cost-effective ways to make the High School Musical part of many children's lives in Asia, and encouraged the Disney Company to customize the actual musical. (2013, pp. 246–247)

China, at the time of writing in 2017, makes up a fifth of the world's population. With this enormous potential consumer base, China is one of the four (besides India, Latin America, and Russia) most important media markets for the Disney Company. The Disney Company collaborates with local media partners, such as CCTV, to produce *High School Musical: China* (Lustyik 2013, p. 248). However, the Chinese adaption in Shanghai was not authentic. The student characters merely imitated American teenagers seen on television and Western-style video clips and YouTube films were emultated to make the musical numbers. As Elley observes: "The majority of the original story line was reduced, and the twelve, rather disconnected musical numbers dominated the movie with little story and character development. While some of the songs became popular, the film had a 'disastrous performance at the Mainland box office', failing to connect with its target audience" (2010; Lustyik 2013, p. 248).

Some might criticize the importation of Western musicals as being like "cultural transplantation," just as Hollywood movies are like "cultural hegemony." Therefore in the twenty-first century, Disney's music-based marketing strategy exemplifies the contemporary situation of global media business. Lustyik doubts that "(e)ven if Disney's customized and hybrid media products, such as a localized soundtrack or regional dance competition, might be developed based on the interests of specific cultures" (2013, p. 250), such media products still "have intertextual traces of an increasingly standardized global media industry" (Kraidy 2005, p. 115). Taking the Disney example, we can learn lessons from the Western and Broadway musicals. Of course, it is better to keep the merits, but not to standardized so much that the joy and the unique cultural characteristics are lost.

Some Chinese Musicals in Hong Kong and China

China's multi-ethnic cultural styles are good for developing the musical, a combination total artwork. While Western musicals cast influence upon China, some Chinese artists also work hard to invent original Chinese musicals, many of which have received recognition and popularity. For example, *Snow Wolf Lake* (1997), performed by the well-known popular Hong Kong singer Jacky H. Cheung (張學友) has achieved overwhelming success due to Cheung's stardom (Tuan 2016 at ATHE).

Among the many that have contributed to the development of the Chinese musical, CCTV's multimedia musical *Song of Film* (2005) really grabbed people's attention; as did *Golden Sand* in Sichuan, *Golden Voice Zhou Xuan*, and *I Am Crazy for Songs*, all full of Shanghai style (Chiu 2009: 43). Learning from Western and Broadway musical, China also produces Chinese original musicals and tours with performances outside of China. For example, China's *Queen of Coquetry* stages in Taiwan. Producer and director Ho Nian (何念), in collaboration with song-writer and singer Hu Yen-Bin (胡彥斌), uses a four-to-eight-person cast—lead actress Si-Wen (司雯) and lead actor Yuan Ye (袁野)—to play the multiple roles in the short scenes in this musical in Taipei.

History and Development of the Musical in Hong Kong and Taiwan

Even though China, Taiwan, and Hong Kong all import Western musicals, Taiwan and Hong Kong both try to infuse national identity with local musical education. Wai-Chung argues that "the transmission of extra-musical learning is essentially a response to the particular needs of these two Chinese historical-social contexts, which require their music curricula to be securely grounded in the ideology of a culturally-based education for 'citizenship'. Despite different approaches to Western-based musical knowledge in schools, Hong Kong and Taiwan attempt to promote a sense of national identity and an essentially Confucian set of moral values as a central goal of school music education" (2003, p. 155).

As discussed in Chapter 8, musical theater in Taiwan has been importing Broadway musicals for different modes of performing in order to stage various aesthetic styles. Few are faithful presentations in English. Most rely on translation from English to Chinese, such as *Kiss Me Nana*, produced by the Godot Theatre and translated from *Kiss Me Kate*. Some of them, such as *Love Ends in Night Shanghai* (2002) adapted from Alexandre Dumas fils' novel *La Dame aux Camelias* and *Running Angel* (2005) adapted from the film *Sister Act* (1992), are opera and film adaptations. Others are original local Asian creations; for example, *See The Sun* (2000) on the Taiwanese aboriginal ethnicity issue and *April Rain* (2007) the Taiwanese musical on the Hakka composer Deng Yu-Hsien's love story under the Japanese colonialization.

Godot Theatre's Restaging of Kiss Me Nana

as we have already discussed at length, most musicals staged in Taiwan rely on translation and adaptation, especially with the majority translating English into Chinese.

From *Kiss Me Kate* to *Kiss Me Nana*, and the Chinese version of *Rent*, the musical theater in Asia has demonstrated its ability to stage not just the Broadway musicals in English, but also original musicals in Asian languages to illustrate the multicultural, intercultural, and multi-linguistic situation in Taiwan.

CASE STUDY: *MOUNTAINS AND SEAS* 《山海經傳》

The musical *Mountains and Seas* (premiered 2013, restage May 2017, Taipei) is directed by Liang, Chi-Ming, artistic director of Godot Theatre and a professor at National Taiwan Normal University (NTNU). The script is an adaptation of the literary work *The Classic of Mountains and Seas* written by Gao Xing-Jian, the 2000 Nobel Prize in Literature winner. According to Liang in the "Director's Interpretation of the Chinese Rock

Musical *Mountains and Seas*,"[2] this rock and roll musical is different from anything he had done before. There is no obvious protagonist in the whole play, but similar to the "excerpts/highlights from opera" (折子戲) in the traditional Chinese opera, each scene can be an independent story. Therefore the music in each scene also has its own independent characteristic. Music by Chris Babida (鮑比達1950–), the professional musician born in Hong Kong, active in Hong Kong and Taiwan is not dull, but popular and good. The lyrics by Chen Le-Jung (1962–) are determined by the words, meanings, and rhythms. Some music composed by Babida contains complex counterpoint and harmony, so Chen carefully digs into each word to check if the lyric will fully represent each character to show the tension of the drama. To honor the Nobel Prize Laureate Gao, NTNU invites the excellent talents in all fields, including dance choreography, costume, projection, technology, and lighting design, to produce this high artistic level production. The cast (with some major characters in Cast A and Cast B) are the masters students who have to pass an audition before being recruited from the professional fields of acting, singing, and dance in the Departments of Performing Arts. The talented actors' and actresses' singing and dancing helps them to convincingly present the Chinese mythical characters through vivid imagery.

I argue that, by staging this legendary myth through spectacle, the issues of love, sexuality, and wars can be visually represented in a more interesting and fascinating way, to meet the requirements of today's multimedia high-technology savvy audiences. With the aid of projection technology, to show the scenes in which there are ten suns in the sky, Hero Hou-Yi shoots down the nine suns by the mise-en-scène of fighting and choreography on stage. This use of spectacle also enables the bird to use stones to attempt to fill up the sea and Chang-Er's ascent to the Moon, and so on.

Love, sexuality, and wars can also be manifested by spectacle. For example, in the love at first sight scene we see the pursuit, flirtation, and sexual chemistry between Hero Hou-Yi and Fufei, Goddess of Luo Water, Neptune's daughter. Their sexual pleasure and jouissance is later symbolized by the dancers' alluring dance on the down stage. The wars between Yan Emperor's general tribe chief Chi-Yo and his soldiers and the Yellow Emperor's troupe, the fierce group fighting and violent action, the big stage design of the two white mountain towers, and the ancient Chinese fable stories and myths are impressively presented to the audience through spectacle (Fig. 9.1).

[2] Special thanks go to Director Liang, Chi-Ming for his generous offer me with his interpretation notes in Chinese and the script in Chinese.

Fig. 9.1 The wars between Yan Emperor's general tribe chief Chi-Yo and his soldiers and the Yellow Emperor's troupe. (Courtesy of NTNU)

Spectacle, Plot, Song, Dance, Stage Design, and Stage Device

Spectacle in *Mountains and Seas* includes the projection of the Scrim in the beginning of the performance to show the very beginning of the earth where Nu Wa (女媧, Goddess Mother Earth in Chinese mythology) appeared from the mirror and used five colorful stones to repair the sky and cultivate the earth. When Nu Wa lay down on the ground to sing, the group actors used long white clothes to simulate the snake tail. Afterwards, Nu Wa ascended high to the air with the aid of the suspension machine system, and the rotating stage turned, then the crowds of people went onto stage. What a spectacle to show the amazing mise-en-scène with such energy! Moreover, the two to three white irregular, sharp mountain forms had tube-like columns to symbolize the heaven where Emperor Handsome, his two Goddess wives, ten Suns sons, and twelve Moons daughters lived. In architecture, columns are usually intended to add grandeur and status. Act 1 ends with the spectacle of Nu Wa ascending into the air (on a hanging wire) to take the air cloud car (Fig. 9.2).

Act 2 starts while the rotating stage changes direction to present the scene of Heaven. Emperor Handsome and Colorful Bird (played by an

Fig. 9.2 Nu Wa (女媧, Goddess Mother Earth in Chinese mythology) ascended into the air, with the aid of the suspension machine system, and the rotating stage turned, then the crowds of people went on stage. (Courtesy of NTNU)

actress) appear to narrate how chaotic it is with the ten naughty Suns sons. Then the Scrim falls down to show the populace on the earth suffering from the heat caused by the ten Suns appearing simultaneously. The dragon car appears in the sky and Emperor Handsome, angry with his sons' reckless and irresponsible behavior, gives Hou-Yi the bow to order him to stop it. The three-arm bridges are lowered down to the earth. The ten Suns are dancing and playing everywhere, causing the people who can't tolerate the heat to run away. Without listening to Hou-Yi's advice to go back to Heaven, nine Suns are shot down by him one by one. Ten bright golden lights symbolize the ten Suns. When they fade, the only remaining Sun left begs Hou-Yi not to kill him. All the people on the earth feel cool and, cheering up, are grateful for Hou-Yi's help. However, Chang-Er, Hou-Yi's wife, is scared that Emperor Handsome will scold and punish Hou-Yi for killing his nine sons. Using clever lighting design, the Scrim shows that Heaven's Gate is closed to punish Hou-Yi by exiling on the mortals' earth without being able to return to heaven and immortality. The Scrim falls down and, with the technological projection of the giant Moon, this scene ends.

As I mentioned earlier, the sexual scene between Hou-Yi and River Queen is romantically and lustfully represented with the spectacle of the symbolic group of chorus girls dancing and waving their long white sleeves. Moreover, the ancient big war in Chinese mythology between Yan Emperor and Yellow Emperor is a marvelous visualization though spectacle. The songs are contemporary, with postmodern commentary. For instance, satirically, Hou-yi is eventually killed by the populace because of his violence. Near the end of the performance, both sides sing their songs, each from their distinctive perspective. Is this history or his story? Who's story? Legitimacy belongs to the winner. Losers are always in the wrong. Whether one will become a king or an outlaw depends on whether he is successful or not. Therefore, we cannot help but ask from whose perspective is this interpretation?

Conclusion

There is no doubt that spectacles such as the Ziegfeld-style parade, the magnificent *Showboat*, and mega musicals can be vivid enough to impress the audience. In Chinese musical, successful adaptation from the Western and Chinese well-known classics can make the familiar stories much more accessible to the audiences. Sexuality and love attract spectators. Thus, in the e-era, unlike Aristotle, who claims that spectacle is the least important part of a play, with the strong impact of movies, virtual reality, computer games, live television shows, YouTube, social media such as Facebook and Twitter, digital technologies, smart phones, and so on upon our daily lives, theater has inevitably given spectacle a much higher status. For example, the Blue Man Group, in their 2013 performance in Boston, did not just play the drums, but also used three big iPads on stage and employed a variety lot of visual digital magic.

Just as in the spectacular spectacle in Las Vegas, the Chinese musical has integrated local language, lyrics, adaptation, wit, music, melody, singing, dancing and acting, stage design, costume design, lighting design, choreography, and architecture, to produce the whole artwork. It has also attempted to use spectacle, with adaptation and sexuality in the plot, to amaze audiences.

By means of multimedia, technology, and spectacles, the themes of literary studies in Gao's Nobel Literature Prize works are now visually accessible to audiences. Through the hypermedia of Internet, virtual reality, projection, and so on, the hypertext of ancient Chinese mythology, oral tradition, narrator's retelling, Gao's literary work, and this rock Chinese musical can be presented. As John Kenrick in the book *Musical Theatre: A History* says: "Disney had invented the *corporate musical,* a genre of shows built, produced, and managed by multifunctional entertainment corporations" (2015, p. 362),. Perhaps the Chinese musical can also try to achieve not only the artistic goals, but also the commercial marketing. *Mountains and Seas* has been touring abroad and has been performed at the Edinburgh Fringe Festival. By performing abroad and attending the noteworthy international theater festivals, the visibility of Chinese musicals will increase and box-office sales will improve. However, the Chinese musical definitely needs to maintain vitality, spirit, spontaneous humanity, and self-reflective commentary to keep making progress.

Translocally in Asia, China, Hong Kong, and Taiwan have learned from Western and Broadway musicals to invent their own Chinese musicals by adaptating from Western and Chinese classics. In the case study of the Chinese musical *Mountains and Seas* (May 2017, Taipei), adapted from the Nobel Prize winner Gao's novel, the spectacles are beneficial to present the scenes of wars and sexuality. Despite some cuts from Gao's original work, the stage score music by Chris Babida, the lyrics by Chen Le-Jung, dance, and acting under director Liang, Chi-Ming's ingenious total theater artwork, in collaboration with the live orchestra, produce this Chinese rock musical adaptation that delights audiences with its fantastic spectacles.

Bibliography

Bay-Cheng, Sarah. "Digital Historiography and Performance." *Theatre Journal.* Vol. 68. Number 4. Dec. 2016, pp. 507–527.
Elley, D. "Disney High School Musical China." 'Review.' *Film Business Asia.* 2010, 10 December.
Ho, W. C. "Democracy, citizenship and extra-musical learning in two Chinese Communities: Hong Kong and Taiwan." *Compare: A Journal of Comparative and International Education.* 33(2), 2003, pp. 155–171.
Liang, Chi-Ming. "Director's Interpretation of the Chinese Rock Musical *Mountains and Seas.*" (In Chinese). March, 2016.
Liang, Chi-Ming. Script of the Chinese Rock Musical *Mountains and Seas.*" (In Chinese). June 19, 2013.
Kenrick, John. *Musical Theatre: A History.* New York and London: Bloomsbury Academic, 2015.
Kraidy, Marwan. *Hybridity, Or the Cultural Logic of Globalization.* Philadelphia: Temple University Press, 2005.

Kun, F., Pratt, K., Provine, R. C., & Thrasher, A. "A discussion on Chinese National Musical Traditions." *Asian Music*. 12(2), 1981, pp. 1–16.
Landow, George and Delany, Paul. "Hypertext, Hypermedia and The History of The Text." In Randall Packer and Ken Jordan eds. *Multimedia: From Wagner to Virtual Reality*. New York and London: W. W. Norton & Company, 2001, pp. 225–238.
Lustyik, Katalin. "Disney's High School Musical: Music makes the world go 'round.'" *Interactions: Studies in Communication & Culture*. Volume 4 Number 3, 2013, pp. 239–253.
Packer, Randall. "The *Gesamtkunstwerk* and Interactive Multimedia." *The Aesthetics of The Total Artwork*. Eds. Anke Finger and Danielle Follett. Baltimore: The Johns Hopkins University Press, 2011, pp. 155–167.
邱爱金. <浅析中国原创音乐剧的发展现状>《音樂天地》2009 (3), pp. 43–45.
———.   <浅析西方音乐剧对中国音乐剧发展的影响>《音樂天地》2008(11), pp. 59–60.

CHAPTER 10

The Abject, Murder, and Sex in *The Great Buddha+*

Abstract Instead of the telescope in Alfred Hitchcock's *Rear Window*, director Hsin-yao Huang in this black-and-white film *The Great Buddha+* (10) uses the car dashcam videos to present the voyeurism of the abject in this digital era. Unlike the two maids who make a sadomasochistic ritual attempt to murder their madam in Jean Genet's play *The Maids*, the two nobodies Belly Bottom (played by Chen Chu-Sheng) and Prickle (played by Chuang Yi-Zeng) discover the murder by Prickle's rich boss Huang Chi-Wen (played by Deon Dai). Visual pleasure, scopophilia, and representation of women are all explored. Film techniques present the oppression of the rich the powerful, the huge gap between the rich and the poor, and the farce and absurdity of life.

Keywords *The Great Buddha+* • Abject • Voyeurism • Scopophilia • Representation of women

MOTIVATION AND INTRODUCTION

Following the writing style of Marvin Carlson, the famous American theater professor and critic, in his latest book *10,000 Nights: Highlights from 50 Years of Theatre-Going*, I'd like to write this book chapter from my personal experience. I have such empathy with the characters who suffer and are murdered in the black-and-white semi-film noir *The Great Buddha+* (the title reflects the iPhone + Plus) that I have been haunted by the ghosts who were murdered in the film ever since I saw the film at the end of October 2017. Last night I didn't sleep until around 2 a.m. and then I had a nightmare in which I was possessed by the female character Madame Yeh who, having been murdered and hidden inside the giant statue of the great Buddha, was crying "why did you killed me?" (Fig. 10.1).

I couldn't sleep after that, so I got up in the early morning. My first thought was that I needed to write about the film to share the obsession with you. After coffee, breakfast, and playing the piano to try to calm down and think more rationally, I'd like to tell you how it is possible for that small-budget film to have the amazing power to stimulate many people's emotions. I have watched many films as a theater professor and film critic, but I haven't seen the local films produced by Taiwan since *Cape No. 7*, a smash hit at the box office in 2008. However, this local film *The Great Buddha+* directed by Hsin-yao Huang (1973–) born in Tainan, Taiwan, impressed not just me and most people, but also got five awards (including the Best New Director, the Best Adapted Screenplay (Hsin-yao Huang), the Best Cinematography (Mong-Hong Chung, under his usual pseudonym as Nagao Nakashima), the Best Original Film Score (Sheng-Xiang Lin), and the Best Original Film Song (Sheng-Xiang Lin, lyrics/performer)

Fig. 10.1 The murder scene. (Courtesy of Photographer Liu, Chen-hsiang)

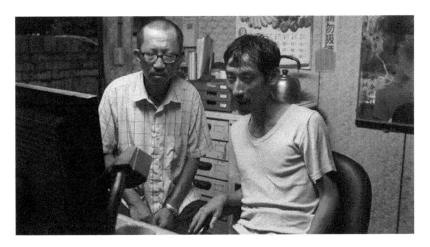

Fig. 10.2 The two nobodies Belly Bottom (played by Chen Chu-Sheng) (right) and Prickle (played by Chuang Yi-Zeng) (left) in *The Great Buddha+* watch Prickle's rich boss having sex in his car on the dashcam videos. (Courtesy of Creamfilm Production)

for the song "To Have, or Not To Have") in the Golden Horse Award Ceremony (the highest film award in Asia, on a par with the Oscars in the US) in 2017.

As a tribute to the telescope in Alfred Hitchcock's *Rear Window*, Director Huang and Producer DP Chung Mong-hong use the car dashcam videos to present voyeurism of the abject in this digital era (Fig. 10.2).

In Jean Genet's play *The Maids* there is a sadomasochistic attempt by two maids to murder their employer Madame. In contrast, the two nobodies Belly Bottom (played by Chen Chu-Sheng) and Prickle (played by Chuang Yi-Zeng) in *The Great Buddha+* don't plan a murder but discover one. They come across a murder committed by Pricke's rich boss Huang Chi-Wen (played by Deon Dai) and the social injustice is that they cannot even accuse him, being forced to keep silent, or killed and hidden.

Plot, Characters, Theme, Language, Rhythm, Spectacle, Music

The theme of this film is social injustice and the sharp contrast between the corrupting wealthy and the very poor who live at the bottom of society (Fig. 10.3).

Fig. 10.3 Poor Belly Bottom lives in poverty. (Courtesy of Photographer Liu, Chen-hsiang)

The plot involves the poor Belly Bottom, who works as a recycling collector during the day, and his only friend Pickle, another poor man who works as a night security guard at a bronze statue factory for his boss Mr. Huang Chi-Wen, accidentally discovering a murder. At nights, Belly Bottom brings the porn magazines he collects during the day to Prickle's small security room in the front of gate of the factory. Flicking through these is Pickle's greatest pleasure in life. In their dull and boring lives, they can only afford to have late night cold snacks, which Belly Bottom picks up from the convenience store trash, and watch television. One day when the television is out of order, Belly Bottom persuades Pickle into taking Boss Huang's peeping Tom car dashcam videos for their voyeuristic pleasure. After that, their nighttime entertainment is watching the rich boss' private sex life. In the cinema movie theater, the spectators also see in the film the rich businessmen and powerful politicians' sex and wine party in the big Jacuzzi at their private club (Fig. 10.4).

Fig. 10.4 The rich businessmen and powerful politicians' sex and wine party in the big Jacuzzi in their private club. (Courtesy of Creamfilm Production)

In contrast, the poor men's basic needs can only be met by their perverse peeping. Women serve as sex toys to be sacrificed, for example, the middle-age woman Madame Yeh is abandoned and cruelly murdered. The ghosts' accusations (after being murdered by the car accident, Belly Bottom's voice off-screen, and the knocking sound from Madame Yeh's ghost inside the giant statue of the great Buddha in the huge Buddhism religious collective chanting praying ceremony gathered by a lot of Buddhists) make the viewers speechless and sad (Fig. 10.5).

Yet the religious ceremony is just a front covering an underhanded land transaction. Even if some of the audience may find the ghosts' accusation preposterous, Director Huang wants to present the view that "isn't life itself a farce?" (IMDb). I think that Huang uses this comedy film to reflect the absurdity of life and the cruelty of social reality.

Fig. 10.5 The monks' and the crowd's lengthy chanting in the ritual is stopped by the gradually louder and louder strange sound coming from the inside of the Big Buddha where Madame Yeh knocks to cry out for justice. (Courtesy of Photographer Liu, Chen-hsiang)

THEORY AND COMMENTS

This film describes the poor characters' lives at the bottom of the society. Thus, I apply the theories of Psychoanalysis and Postcolonialism, such as Julia Kristeva's notion of "abjection," Homi Bhabha's postcolonial concept of the "abject," voyeurism, and the related conjunctures to interpret the characters of Belly Bottom and Prickle from the perspective of the abject to accuse the rich and powerful of oppression, look at the huge gap between the rich and the poor and the subtle human nature.

Kristeva's concept of abjection, based on Sigmund Freud's Psychoanalysis as therapy, the *Three Essays on the Theory of Sexuality*, and Jacques Lacan's psychoanalytic theories, is used commonly and effectively to explain popular cultural narratives of horror and misogyny. The men being rejected with disgust and hatred to be looked down on as trash; the term "abjection" literally means "the state of being cast off." Nobodies in a small town in southern Taiwan, such as Belly Bottom and Prickle, are cast off by society. Yet Belly Bottom would degrade Prickle. Belly Bottom appears to be killed by accident, but actually he is murdered to cover Huang's previous murder of Madame Yeh (played by Ting Kuo-Lin), whom he had used for sex for years under the pretense of one day marrying her.

French feminist psychoanalyst and scholar Julia Kristeva, in *Powers of Horror*, depicts subjective horror (abjection) as the feeling when an individual experiences, or is confronted by (both mentally and physically as a body experience), what Kristeva terms one's "corporeal reality," or a disruption distinguished from self and other. The concept of abjection can be described as the process in which one separates one's sense of self—be it physical and biological, social, or cultural—from that which one considers intolerable and infringes upon one's self, otherwise, known as the abject. The abject is, as such, the "me that is not me" (Wikipedia). So, we can see the horror between the "me, that is not me" in the abjection.

As for voyeurism and scopophilia, Freud in *Three Essays on Sexuality* indicates that looking itself is a source of pleasure. In the reverse formation, there is also pleasure in being looked at. Freud isolated scopophilia as one of the component instincts of sexuality, existing independently of the erotogenic zones as sexual drives. Laura Mulvey in "Visual Pleasure and Narrative Cinema" combines Freud's psychoanalysis theory with film theory, in which the mechanism creates the representation of women in film. Sarah Bay-Cheng indicates that Mulvey "considered the pleasure film creates through three interrelated psychoanalytic experiences: scopophilia (the pleasure of looking), voyeurism (the pleasure from looking at sexual acts), and ego libido (the formation of identification)" (2005, p. 164).

With regard to visual pleasure, scopophilia, and representation of women in films, in my observation, women's bodies, and sometimes those sexual alluring feminine body parts such as breasts, legs, lips, eyes, hips, and so on, are specifically for the male gaze. For example, in one film frame Madame Yeh's tight dress is designed to show her curvaceous body and is presented as a contrast to the dark background in the black-and-white film. This example adeptly explains Freud's theory of men's castration anxiety. The provocation of the woman, with her lack of a penis, threatens the male spectator, therefore she is instead often fetishized on screen in films; represented only as a part, not the whole, such as a face or a pair of legs or breasts. In my view, this is not only to relieve the male spectator's anxiety, but also to arouse the heterosexual male spectator's desire and the female spectator's imitation.

INTERCULTURAL COMPARISON

In Jean Genet's play *The Maids* the two maids Solange and Claire secretly conduct their imaginary sadomasochistic ritual ceremony of murdering their Madame while she is away. Genet roughly adapted the actual brutal murders carried out by the infamous Christine and Léa Papin sisters who murdered their employer and her daughter in France in 1933.

In the film *The Great Buddha+*, the two nobodies Belly Bottom and Prickle discover the murder Prickle's boss Huang has committed while watching his car dashcam videos.

In historical literary review, Kuan-Hsing Chen in "Taiwanese New Cinema" in *World Cinema* writes: "The crucial point about Taiwan New Cinema is not so much the originality of its aesthetic forms as its strategic ideological function within the wider cultural history of Taiwan and, more precisely, its historical turn on the discovery and construction of the 'Taiwanese self'" (2000, p. 174).

FILM TECHNIQUES

Numerous film techniques, such as voice over, elaborate echoes, close ups, pan shots, composition, newsreel, and so on, are employed. Using the high angle shot, the position of witness Belly Bottom's dead body made it look accidental—as if he had fallen into the big dry ditch to his death while drunk—when, actually, he was run over by a car to prevent him from divulging Huang's murderous secret. After the shabby funeral band march, Prickle and the convenience store's employer Potato (played by Lin Yu-Chih, with stage name Nàdòu (Natto)—total only 5 people attend the funeral—suddenly come across the water-flooded ditch that is blocking their way. The voice of the dead Belly Bottom then speaks, telling them that he has created the flood to prevent them from going any further; that this is as good enough a place as any for his send-off. I think that the water represents the river separating the dead and the living (Fig. 10.6).

Fig. 10.6 The voice of the dead Belly Bottom. (Courtesy of Creamfilm Production)

There are many elaborate parallels from the beginning to the end of this film; for instance, in the middle of the film, a newsreel on TV shows Belly Bottom being caught by the bully policemen and forced to have his photo taken while being hit on the ground. The photo is taken close up and shows his face twisted in pain. Ironically, that is the only photo of Belly Bottom, so, near the end of the film his friends have to use that as his funeral portrait.

CONCLUSION

Having started his career shooting documentary films, Director Hsin-yao Huang in this first drama feature film effectively uses parody comedy (satire) to depict the social realism of the nobodies' poor, marginal status: oppressed by the rich and the powerful. It is ironic that the powerful politician can oppress the policeman to force him to drop his investigation of the rich businessman murder suspect Huang with these threatening words: "the grass on your grave would already be this high!" (Fig. 10.7).

The pathos of Taiwan's underclass is portrayed well by Huang's direction. This black-and-white film, *The Great Buddha+*, is an extraordinary, excellent film that is worth seeing. It also provides a perfect contrast the color film *The Bold, The Corrupt, and The Beautiful*, discussed in Chapter 11. Both films were first shown in 2017 and criticize the corruption of wealth and politics. These artistic films reflect the social, economic, and

Fig. 10.7 Ironically, the powerful politician can threaten the policeman into dropping his investigation of the rich businessman. (Courtesy of Creamfilm Production)

political current situation in Taiwan; the former from the perspective of nobodies at the abject bottom of society, the latter from the view of somebodies who have money and power at the top of society. All the events are adapted from real social scandal and murder events happening in translocality in Taiwan, Hong Kong, and China.

Bibliography

Carlson, Marvin. *10,000 Nights: Highlights from 50 Years of Theatre-Going*. Ann Arbor: University of Michigan Press, 2017.
Chen, Kuan-Hsing. "Taiwanese New Cinema." *World Cinema: Critical Approaches*. Ed. John Hill and Pamela Church Gibson. Oxford and New York: Oxford University Press, 2000.
Sala, Massimiliano. Ed. *From Stage to Screen: Musical Films in Europe and United Stages (1927–1961)*. Italy: Brepols, 2012.
Suh, Sharon A. *Silver Screen Buddha: Buddhism in Asian and Western Film*. USA: Bloomsbury Academic, 2015.
Mulvey, Laura. "Visual Pleasure and Narrative Cinema." +…
Bay-Cheng, Sarah. "The Influence (and Problems) of Feminist Film Theory in Theater Criticism." *Theater and Film: A Comparative Anthology*. New Haven and London: Yale University Press, 2005.

WEBSITES

Toronto International Film Festival. http://www.tiff.net/tiff/the-great-buddha/ Retrieved on Dec. 12, 2017.

Film Review: 'The Great Buddha+' http://variety.com/2017/film/reviews/the-great-buddha-review-1202566032/ Retrieved on Dec. 12, 2017.

USNEWS. https://www.usnews.com/news/entertainment/articles/2017-10-02/the-great-buddha-grabs-10-golden-horse-nominations. Retrieved on Dec. 12, 2017.

2017 Taipei Film Festival. http://eng.taipeiff.taipei/Latest_s.aspx?FwebID=281a5969-697e-47f0-9e68-72031fc796a6&NewsID=240. Retrieved on Dec. 12, 2017.

IMDb. http://www.imdb.com/title/tt7010412/plotsummary?ref_=tt_ov_pl, Retrieved on Dec. 6, 2017.

Wikipedia. https://en.wikipedia.org/wiki/Abjection. Retrieved on Dec. 6, 2017.

CHAPTER 11

Sex, Money, Calculation, and Manipulation in Politics in *The Bold, The Corrupt, and The Beautiful*

Abstract The nuance of the film techniques in this color thriller is explored in the frame of female gothic monstrous horror. Control, ambition, desire, and lust eventually destroy Madame Tang's relationships with her own family, and the story ends in a social realism tragedy. The theme is the ugliness of the human heart, which is even more terrible than ghosts and darker than corrupted politics. The ten female characters are cunning and the three Tang protagonists are calculating and manipulative. The "abnormal, or monstrous, manifestations of the child–parent tie" transforms the standard patriarchy into the female gothic monster loveless hatred relationship. Since Taiwanese New Cinema was developed in the 1980s, I think there is not only Bildungsroman narrative expression, but also the identification swift from China to Taiwan.

Keywords *The Bold, The Corrupt, and The Beautiful* • Thriller • Gothic • Monstrous • Bildungsroman

INTRODUCTION

The Great Buddha+ and *The Bold, The Corrupt, and The Beautiful* (which both received several awards in the Golden Horse Awards) concern sex, money, corruption, politics, and murders.

I'll analyze and comment on the nuance of the thriller style film in the theoretical frame of the female gothic monstrous horror. The cunning and the monstrous are shown in the film *The Bold, The Corrupt, and The Beautiful*, which received Best Drama Picture, Best Actress, and Best Supporting Actress in the 2017 Golden Horse Awards and the Best Picture voted by the audiences (Fig. 11.1).

THEME, PLOT, CHARACTERS, LANGUAGE, MUSIC

The Bold, The Corrupt, and The Beautiful is a dark, cold, and cruel story set in the 1980s in Taiwan. Following her general husband's death Madame Tang (played by Actress Hui, Yin-Hung from Hong Kong) is working as an arts, antiques, and jewelry broker. She lives with her daughter Tang Ning (played by Wu, Ke-Sin), who is in her thirties, and her granddaughter Tang Chen, who is fourteen-years old (played by Wen-Chi) and whom Madame Tang pretends is her younger daughter in order to save face. Madame Tang colludes with and mediates between the government and private businesses for the interest and benefit of her all-female family. However, an attempt to buy and sell an antique statue of the Buddha does not go according to plan, and her good friends the Lin family become victims of a gruesome murder. Control, ambition, desire, and lust eventually destroy Tang's relationships with her own family in a social realism tragedy.

All of the ten women characters in this film are calculating. Madame Tang is so calculating and manipulative that she prostitutes out her daughter to men, including the two Tuan killers Madame Tang hires from Burma, gangsters, (Fig. 11.2), powerful politicians, and the policeman, to make money and escape from the prison.

Tang Ning protests to Madame Tang: "Am I just like a brand bag for you? When I am young and beautiful, you take me to show off and make use of me. When I am torn to be used up, you look for the new brand bag" (the young Tang Chen). Madame Tang treats Tang Ning like a tool. Madame buys a sexy black lace nightgown for Tang Ning so that she may seduce the policeman investigating the Liu family murders, telling her "you are on the surface a princess, but indeed live the life of a handmaid." Madame Tang uses her own daughter Tang Ning for numerous schemes even being so cruel as to kill her to avoid the scandal being revealed.

The theme of this film the ugliness of the human heart, which is more disturbing than ghosts and darker than the corruption of politics. Director and Screenwriter Yang Ya-Jie's tagline for this film is: "The most horrible thing in the world is not the impending punishment for the crime, but the future with no love." Although both of the mothers tell their daughters that "I'm doing this for your own good," in fact, they just want to control

SEX, MONEY, CALCULATION, AND MANIPULATION IN POLITICS IN *THE*... 153

Fig. 11.1 The poster of the film *The Bold, The Corrupt, and The Beautiful*. The three leading actresses are from Hong Kong and Taiwan. The youngest actress is studying and pursuing her career in China now. (Courtesy of Yang Ya-Jie)

Fig. 11.2 The young fourteen-year-old Tang Chen watches from the window while Tang Ning is having sex with the two gangsters. (Courtesy of Yang Ya-Jie)

their daughters, which in turn makes the daughters rebellious toward the cruelness they have suffered. When Tang Ning attempts to take her daughter Tang Chen and run away from Madame Tang and take the fishing boat to Burma, Tang Ning uses handcuffs to force Tang Chen to go with her. In response to her mother Tang Ning's "I'm doing this for your own good," the young Tang Chen spits on Tang Ning's face and states "you are both the same."

In this film, numerous languages, including Mandarin, Taiwanese dialect, Cantonese, Japanese, Hakka, and Taiwanese Aboriginal, are used to show the multicultural social phenomenon in Taiwan. The visual culture represented by the poster/painting is spectacular, vivid, and shocking in its depiction of the circular life cycle of karma and revenge between the three females in the Tang family.

The music in this film is arranged by Ke Chi-Hou, who mixes Taiwanese opera, Taiwanese storytelling and singing (with songs such as Yang's "Injustice sunk into the Sea with Heart Discontent"), Nanguan (South Tube), and Beiguan (North Tube) with Western orchestration, like "Carmen" and chorus singing. In the scene where Madame Tang is throwing a big party, with a buffet and pavilion banquet, for the unveiling of a portrait of Madame Wang (the Minister of Legislative Yuan's wife), the singers and dancers perform in the large garden. The song titles, for example, the Taiwanese song and lyrics "Innocent Youth Dream" (<純情青春夢>) sung by Singer Hsiu-lan Maya, serve as the hints and tones for the development of the film. The last song "Hell" sounds creepy.

THEORY

The Cunning and the Monstrous

As mentioned earlier, I think that the ten female characters in this film are cunning and the three protagonists in the Tang family are cunning and monstrous. In Clare Connors's book *Literary Theory: A Beginner's Guide*, she documents that in "its treatment of women" the eclectic works of male writers, such as Goethe, Spencer and Swift "falls into a simple, pernicious, either/or structure, in which women are cast either as 'angels' or as 'monsters'" (2010). In this vein, the women in this film are like evil monsters.

Female writing, according to Sandra Gilbert and Susan Gubar, is "cunning in its very simplicity." Although this film's script writer and director Yang is a man, when he was interviewed on TV and asked why he is able to so astutely and sensitively write about and direct the female characters' calculating and manipulative mindset, he answered that he has learned from some female producers.

I apply feminism to exploring the female characters in this film. French feminist critics, for example, Julia Kristeva, Luce Irigaray, and Hélèna Cixous, among others, can rebel in the linguistic system through strategic silence or by *l'écriture féminine*, a feminine writing based on women's subjectivity and body instinct. In this context, Tang Chen's silence while serving water and pouring tea, enables her to watch and learn about the adults' calculating and manipulative mind games—her strategy throughout the teenage development period. She also silently observes her friend's secret love in those triangle scenes (Fig. 11.3).

Tang Chen gradually learns all of Madame Tang's cunning, calculating, and manipulative schemes. For example, when Madame Tang takes her hand to draw the dark red flowers of hell during a Chinese water painting lesson, we see that this is a metaphor for learning to face the unseen horrible without fear. Tang Chen takes on this lesson when she encounters the murders of the Lin family. She leaves her good friend Lin Pien-Pien dying in a hospital bed so that her love opponent is removed. After witnessing her mother Tang Ning's murder by her grandmother Madame Tang, Tang Chen tries to run

Fig. 11.3 The fantasy love triangle scene in the forest. (Courtesy of Yang Ya-Jie)

away by train with Marco, who she's secretly in love with. However, after Marco ruthlessly rapes her and reveals that he is being controlled by both Lin Pien-Pien and her mother Madame Lin who forces him to be her lover by keeping his ID, she is totally heartbroken and desperately jumps out of the train, only to be hit by the train and lose her right leg. Her prosthetic leg, decorated with blue and white porcelain, echoes the learning process and those traumatic physical imprints written forever on the female body.

The female characters can be seen as disfigured, gothic, monstrous, and Frankenstein-like, born of the abnormal child–parent tie. Diane Long Hoeveler uses feminism, post-colonial theory, cultural studies, queer theory, and disability studies to interpret Mary Shelley's *Frankenstein*. According to Hoeveler, Ellen Moers in her *Literary Women*, first coined the term "female gothic" to define what she called a genre written by women, centering on a "young woman who is simultaneously persecuted victim and courageous heroine." Moers's reading of literature is significant "not as a purely cerebral activity, but as one based in the pleasures and pains of the body" (Hoeveler 2004, p. 46). In this film, we do see the *jouissance*, the sexual pleasure of Tang Ning when she is having sex with men, despite being forced by Madame Tang to do so, and pains, such as Tang Chen's loss of her leg—symbolizing the pleasure and pain of the female body.

This film can also be viewed as the "abnormal, or monstrous, manifestations of the child–parent tie" (Hoeveler 2004) and, in so doing, transforms the standard patriarchy family into the female gothic monster hatred relationship without love. The young fourteen-year-old female character Tang Chen can be regarded as the transformation of the male monster Frankenstein, in the perverse child–parent tie and strange fake mother–daughter–sisters' relationships (actually, grandmother–mother–granddaughter relationship) in the matriarchy Tang's all-female family.

The "abnormal, or monstrous, manifestations of the child–parent tie" (Hoeveler 2004) is graphically depicted with visual symbols, such as their family uniform costumes, the paintings of the hell flowers, and the visible manifestation of the oil painting/big prop/poster drawn by the female painter Liu, Yi-Lan. The name of the painting is "Far Away from The Other Shore is the Other Shore Flower." It means that after death, before going across to the Other Shore, there is the dark red hell flower (the Other Shore Flower) shining like ghost fire in Hell.

Director Yang has said that he hates mendacity, so he uses the family wrapped in uniforms to express the strict control, the deceitful culture in which human hearts are corrupted to the core.

The male Yang is good at depicting the cunning and monstrous women's calculating and manipulative schemes. Without a patriarchal father figure, Madame Tang is the dominating monarch of the family. In the case of the Bildungsroman formation novel, from Tang Chen's teenage perspective, it is the learning process of how to become like the cruel Madame Tang.

As Kuan-Hsing Chen writes:

What can be termed as Bildungsroman narrative–expressed in *Ah-Fei* (`Rape Seed', 1983), *The Boys from Fengkuei* (1983), *Growing Up* (1983), *Summer at Grandpa's* (1984), *Dust in the Wind* (1986), *Taipei Story* (1985), *A Time to Live and a Time to Die* (1985), *Banana Paradise* (1989), and *A Brighter Summer Day* (1991)—not only retraced their youth in the memory of the post-war generation, but also charted the trajectories of changing environments, political and economic (2000, p. 175).

I think that not only is there Bildungsroman narrative expression in *The Bold, The Corrupt, and The Beautiful* but also an identification switch from China to Taiwan. We see the protagonist Madame Tang, originally working as a nightclub dancer in Hong Kong, marrying General Tang and migrating from China with the Kuomintang Political Party (led by the former President Chiang Kai-shek) in 1949 to live in Taiwan. Following the trend of Taiwan New Cinema, the focus of this film also moves from poor rural agricultural life to the rich industrial urban society where the greedy rich businessmen collude with the corrupted politicians in illegal land development.

Analysis and Comments, Film Techniques

There are some special film techniques employed in this film. For example, one role is played by two actresses, there are narrators, similar camera shots, parody, newsreel, flash back, lip sync, dubbing, frames-within-frames, and so on. The film starts with a flash back: actress Ke, Chia-Yeh plays the adult role of Tang Chen appearing in the newsreel on TV in the beginning of the film and near the end of the film. Using frames-within-frames, the blind storytelling narrators (including Taiwan treasure Yang Hsiu-ching), in the TV studio within the film frame, tell and comment on Tang's family story (Fig. 11.4).

In the beginning of the film, set in the TV station, the workers guess of the adult Tang Chen that, as the blind storytelling narrator Yang passes by to point, "what she says is to save her." The next setting is in the other TV studio where the two blind storytelling narrators record the live TV program tracing back thirty years ago to tell the Tang family's story of ugly politics, murders, sex, money, greed, and calculating, manipulative humanity. By employing

Fig. 11.4 The blind storytelling narrators (including Taiwan Treasure Yang Hsiu-ching) in the TV studio's frame within the film frame tell and comment on Tang's family story. (Courtesy of Yang Ya-Jie)

this film technique, the two blind storytelling narrators are not just insightful, but use something similar to Bertolt Brecht's "alienation effect" to keep an aesthetic distance while commenting critically on social events.

Some repetitive camera shots in this film—for example, the hospital scenes in the middle of the film and near the end of the film—echo each other.

Lip sync and dubbing are also used to ensure that the actress Wen-Chi (who plays Tang Chen) has pure local pronunciation of Mandarin, Taiwanese, and Japanese.

The cinematography, set design, and art design are extraordinary in their integration of the colorful dark red and dark blue that symbolize the sober, cold, dark corruption of politics colliding with the greed of business. Even the mother–daughter–granddaughter relationship is twisted, cunning, monstrous, calculating, and manipulating: there is no love, but devilish hatred and torture. At last, Madame Tang cannot die peacefully as she wishes, but is forced to live as a vegetable in hospital, relying on the oxygen machine. As Tang Chen holds her hand, we see the green jade bracelet on her wrist, the symbol that she now holds the power. The camera moves back and forth to present Madame Tang's scared enlarged eyeballs, her throat painfully croaking, and Tang Chen's cold, insincere smile that is full of revenge (Fig. 11.5).

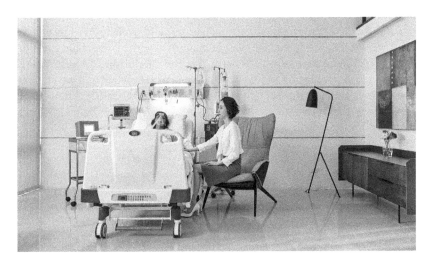

Fig. 11.5   The hospital scene. (Courtesy of Yang Ya-Jie)

It is unsurprising that Tang Chen feels this way, after all she experience the depth of Madame Tang's cruelty when she killed her own daughter Tang Ning, Tang Chen's real mother.

The flaw is that there is a little irrelevant opposition in the camera work. For instance, the intruding two dancers with their faces painted like Japanese Geishas being shown in the background of Tang Ning on the balcony is very strange, absurd, and weird.

Conclusion

Yang is ingenious in his weaving of the real social events that happened in Taiwan, such as the nine murders at Taoyuan County Mayer Liu Ban-yu's mansion (which is still unsolved), political power struggle, illegal land investments, illegal extra-bank loans, gangsters conflicts, and so on, into the fictional cinematic plot. Finally, the locality of Taiwanese culture demonstrates a powerful protest against the corruption of politics and the greed of business, to present either the lives of those with the lowest social standing or the middlemen who are implicated in helping taking bribes in corruption.

Both *The Bold, The Corrupt, and The Beautiful* and *The Great Buddha+* are honest in their message that justice may not come in time to save the innocent. Even the saying "Goodness gets rewards, and badness gets the punishments" cannot really be true in the reality of the ugly world of politics and the dark society of power mechanisms and exchanges of interests. However, at least even the bad people need to face the natural life cycle of getting old and becoming ill. What if the bad cannot die, as Mr. Huang Chi-Wen and Madame Tang wish, but are kept barely alive in an endless torture of seeing the future without love, and the devil beside them. What Yang wants to convey is exactly that—would that perhaps be even worse than the limited prison sentences?

Bibliography

Chen, Kuan-Hsing. "Taiwanese New Cinema." *World Cinema: Critical Approaches*. Ed. John Hill and Pamela Church Gibson. Oxford and New York: Oxford University Press, 2000.

Connors, Clare. *Literary Theory: A Beginner's Guide*. London: Oneworld Publications, 2010.

Hoeveler, Diane. "Frankenstein, Feminism, and Literary Theory," in *The Cambridge Companion to Mary Shelley*. Ed. Esther Schor. Cambridge: Cambridge University Press, 2004: 45–62.

CHAPTER 12

Conclusion

Abstract Contemporary Legend Theatre (CLT)'s *A Midsummer Night's Dream* portrays the Asian dream and local cultural imagination. I explore this Japanese flavor and argue that authentic Japanese cultural roots and Western–Asian interculture impact on Ninagawa's *Hamlet*. *To Send Away Under Escort* with intertextuality of Beijing opera contains nostalgia, local politics, and love. Hakka opera develops to be Hakka musical and Hakka TV drama to reflect the translocal culture promulgated by government's local cultural policy via media. Hakka culture and images are represented theatricality in the film *My Native Land* and in other performances (dance and concert). The development and recent trends of Chinese musical in China, Hong Kong, and Taiwan are explored. Adapted from Nobel Prize winner Gao Xing-Jian's play, the musical *Mountains and Seas* is explored theoretically from translocality and multimedia on spectacle. The film *The Great Buddha+* uses car dashcam videos to present the voyeurism of the abject. The cunning and the monstrous are represented in the film *The Bold, The Corrupt, and The Beautiful*.

Keywords *A Midsummer Night's Dream* • *Hamlet* • Hakka • Chinese musical • *The Great Buddha+* • *The Bold, The Corrupt, and The Beautiful*

This book consists of an Introduction, ten main chapters, and this Conclusion. Most chapters are on intercultural theater performances including Taiwanese, Chinese, and Japanese cultural elements staged in Taiwan. Some are musical performances in Taiwan and Hong Kong.

Chapter 2 "Methodologies: From Postcolonial Feminism and Creolization Toward Translocal" focuses on the theories I use to explore performance and the examples I use throughout the book. Theoretical methodologies, from postcolonialism, feminism, interculturalism, creolization of theories, lead on to the new theory of translocality, combining performance studies with scape and geography, with cultural mobility as the development base.

In Chapter 3 "CLT's *A Midsummer Night's Dream*: Tradition, Modernity, and Translocality", I propose that cultural performances as Asian intercultural Shakespearean performances are deterritorialized, crossing the boundaries of territorial limitation, not limited to the particular styles of Peking opera, *kunju*, *yueju*, Japanese *noh* or *kabuki*, Indian *kathakali*, spoken drama, experimental theater, avant-garde theater, Broadway musical, to name just a few. After all, in the translocal e-era with plentiful information and advanced technology, such as iCloud, big data, robots, artificial intelligence, virtual reality, and so on, we can integrate those useful and practical methods to make progress toward the totality of artistic creation.

Just like some particular trees grow in certain areas, ethnoscapes are about the construction of locality, the particular stylization of Peking opera, profound artistic singing, reciting, acting, and fighting are its essence and requirements. CLT's *A Midsummer Night's Dream*, despite the disappointment of many audiences and critics, should still work on the polish and refinement of the core of the artistic expression of Peking opera. Otherwise, all of the facetious advertisement has no meaning. After CLT's well-acclaimed *Kingdom of Desire* (1986), the audiences and critics expect to see another milestone reached.

Chapter 4 "Yukio Ninagawa's *Hamlet* in Taiwan: Intercultural Representation." Ninagawa employed the cinematic technique of slow motion, freezing movements and sharp lights to show the characters and players' grotesque movement. I think that those designs symbolize the corrupt chaotic politics. Both the Elizabethan classical drama of Shakespeare and the Japanese traditional theater styles like *kabuki* are affinities. Ninagawa's use of spectacles, including the exotic and oriental elements, appeals to the audiences' nostalgia toward Japan in Taiwan. Ninagawa's *Hamlet* (2015) in Taiwan is a representative East–West fusion and intercultural performance. Ninagawa's accomplishments in theater are remembered even after his death in 2016.

CONCLUSION 163

Chapter 5 "Theater Represents Literature: Love and Labor in *To Send Away Under Escort*." This performance fits the common theme of human beings' love, compassion, caring, bonds, empathy, sympathy, family and friendship, emotions and feelings, which are everlasting. Those abstract feelings written in the literature can be visualized by theater performance. Literature can be transformed from different genres, from novel to script, and then into performance through the labor of adaptation and mixed languages in revitalizing Asian performance.

Chapter 6 "Change of Hakka Opera: Ethnicity and Creation in Hakka Musical and Hakka TV Drama" focuses on *My Daughter's Wedding*, a Hakka musical in Taiwan adapted from Shakespeare's *The Taming of the Shrew*, and refers to *The Yang's Ninth Sister*, a Hakka drama performed by the Sin-Yong-Guang Troupe played on TV. The issues of ethnicity and identity are explored to discover the process and draw the conclusion of Hakka opera's shift from tradition to creation.

Chapter 7 "Hakka Culture and Image in Film and Performance" uses three examples to illustrate the issues of Hakka culture and Hakka images, which are explored in the theoretical perspective of cultural mobility and translocality. While theatrical mobility may exist in different adaptations, glocalization can integrate translocal cultures and theatrical performing methods. Hakka culture and images can be visibly seen in cinema and the live performances of drama, dance, and music concert.

Chapter 8 "Irresistible Seduction and Translocal Labor of Musical Theater in Taiwan: From Translation to Multi-Arts" uses several great examples and history to illuminate that, trans across the landscapes, musical theater in Taiwan has paved her way from translocal labor of translation, in the process of adaptation and authenticity, to the production of original multi-arts creations.

Chapter 9 "Spectacle, Adaptation, and Sexuality in Chinese Musicals" points out that in Asia, China, Hong Kong, and Taiwan have learned from Western and Broadway musicals to invent their own Chinese musicals through adaptation from Western and Chinese classics. In the Chinese musical *Mountains and Seas* (May 2017, Taipei), adapted from the Nobel Prize winner Gao's novel, the spectacles are beneficial when presenting the scenes of wars and sexuality. Despite some cuts from Gao's original work, the stage score music by Chris Babida, the lyrics by Chen Le-Jung, dance and acting under director Liang, Chi-Ming's ingenious total theater artwork, collaborated with the live orchestra, this Chinese rock musical *Mountains and Seas* adaptation delights audiences with its fantastic spectacles.

Finally, Chapters 10 and 11 explore the two 2017 Asian films *The Great Buddha+* and *The Bold, The Corrupt, and The Beautiful*, both produced by directors from Taiwan. These films both received several Golden Horse Awards. These last two films to be discussed in the book are concerned with the local and the global issues of politics, sex, power, and corruption, in Taiwan, Hong Kong, and China.

As William Shakespeare says: "All the world's a stage." Through excellent performances explored with the aid of performance and film studies, in the new theoretical frame of translocality, the complexity, beauty, sorrow, farce, absurdity, joy, happiness, love, hatred, and philosophy of life are reflected and represented in translocal Asian theater and film.

BIBLIOGRAPHY

CHAPTER 1

Moers, Ellen. 1978. *Literary Women*. London: The Women's Press.

CHAPTER 2

Appadurai, Arjun. 1996. *Modernity at Large: Cultural Dimensions of Globalization*. Minneapolis and London: University of Minnesota Press.
Felluga, Dino. 2012. "Modules on Baudrillard: On Simulation." *Introductory Guide to Critical Theory*. Purdue U. Access Date: April 2, 2016. https://www.cla.purdue.edu/english/theory/postmodernism/modules/baudlldsimulTnmainframe.html.
Benjamin, Walter. 1936. *Illuminations*. 1969[1936], p. 218, pp. 220–221. "The work of Art in the Age of Mechanical Reproduction." Source: UCLA School of Theater, Film and Television; Translated: by Harry Zohn; Published: by Schocken/Random House, ed. by Hannah Arendt; Transcribed: by Andy Blunden 1998; proofed and corrected Feb. 2005. https://www.marxists.org/reference/subject/philosophy/works/ge/benjamin.htm.
Cheng Fan-Ting. 2013. "Dreamers' Nightmare: The Melancholia of the TaiwaneseCentennial Celebration." *Asian Theatre Journal*. Vol. 30 no.1: Spring, pp. 172–188.
Diamond, Catherine. 1994. "*Kingdom of Desire*: The Three Faces of *Macbeth*." *Asia Theatre Journal* 11, no. 1: 114–133.
———. 1995. "Reflected and Refracted: Metatheatrics in Taiwan." *Journal of Dramatic Theory and Criticism*. Vol. 9, no. 2: 84–96.

Foley, Kathy. 2016. "Book Review." *Modern Asian Theatre and Performance 1900–2000*. Kevin J. Wetmore Jr., Siyuan Liu, and Erin B. Mee. The Modern Drama Anthology of Modern Plays. Eds. Siyuan Liu and Kevin J. Wetmore Jr. *Asian Theatre Journal*. 33, no. 1: 217–220.
Fuchs, Elinor & Chaudhuri, Una. 2002. *Land/Scape/Theater*. Eds. Ann Arbor: The University of Michigan Press.

Chapter 3

CLT. 2016. Program of *A Midsummer Night's Dream*. (Fashion Legend Musical.) Taipei: Contemporary Legend Theatre.
Diamond, Catherine. 1994. "*Kingdom of Desire*: The Three Faces of *Macbeth*." *Asia Theatre Journal* 11, no. 1: 114–133.
———. 1995. "Reflected and Refracted: Metatheatrics in Taiwan." *Journal of Dramatic Theory and Criticism* 9, no. 2: 84–96.
Kim, Kyoung Jae. 2016. "Performance Review. The Sixth International Theatre Olympics in Beijing." *Asian Theatre Journal*, vol. 33, no. 1: 198–202.
Huang, Alexander [Alexa]. 2005. "Impersonation, Autobiography, and Cross-Cultural Adaptation: Lee Kuo-Hsiu's *Shamlet*." *Asian Theatre Journal* 22, no. 1: 122–137.
———. 2009. *Chinese Shakespeares: Two Centuries of Cultural Exchange*. New York: Columbia University Press.
Schechner, Richard. 2002. "Simulation, Jean Baudrillard." *Performance Studies: An Introduction*. London and New York: Routledge, pp. 117–122.
Steger, B. Manfred. 2014. "Interview with Appadurai." *Globalizations*, vol. 11 (4): 481–490.
Tuan, Iris Hsin-chun. 2007. *Alternative Theater in Taiwan: Feminist and Intercultural Approaches*. New York: Cambria Press.
Wang, An-Chi. 2003. 《寂寞沙洲冷—周正榮京劇藝術》("Lonely Cold Alluvion—Chou Cheng-Jung's Peking Opera Art."), Yilan: National Center for Traditional Arts.
Wetmore, J. Kevin, Liu, Siyuan, and Mee, B. Erin. 2014. *Modern Asian Theatre and Performance 1900–2000*. London and New York.

Websites

Kuo, Chiang-sheng. 2016. 《莎翁的喜劇,吳興國的悲劇》 (Shakespeare's Comedy, Wu Hsing-kuo's Tragedy) *ARTalks*, 28 March, http://talks.taishinart.org.tw/juries/kjs/2016032801, accessed 8 June 2016.
Tsai, Shao-chien. 2016. 《京劇基因打造音樂莎劇 當代傳奇譜時尚《仲夏夜之夢》》 (*Jingju* Gene Creates Musical Shakespeare. CLT Composes Fashion

A Midsummer Night's Dream). http://www.ettoday.net/news/20160324/668503.htm, accessed 12 June 2016.

Zhang, Xiao-xiong. 2016.《饒了莎翁吧!》(Give Shakespeare a Break). *ARTalks*, 25 March. http://talks.taishinart.org.tw/juries/xxz/2016032501, accessed 12 June 2016.

CHAPTER 4

Brokering, Jon M. "Ninagawa Yukio's Intercultural *Hamlet*: Parsing Japanese Iconography." *Asian Theatre Journal*, 2007, Vol. 24 (2), pp. 370–397.

Ellis, Samantha. G2: Arts: 'Some people can't let it go': As Yukio Ninagawa's sixth production of *Hamlet* opens, Samantha Ellis asks directors why they return to the play. (Guardian Features Pages). Yukio Ninagawa, Richard Eyre, Trevor Nunn And Jonathan Kent. *The Guardian* (London, England), Sept 29, 2004, p.11.

Hickling, Alfred. "Saturday review: Arts: Doctor Noh: Japan's traditional theatre is so dull it sends entire audiences to sleep. If anyone can spice things up, it's Yukio Ninagawa." Alfred Hickling meets the great ashtray-flinging director. (Guardian Saturday Pages). *The Guardian* (London, England), May 19, 2001, p.5.

Im, Yeeyon. "The pitfalls of intercultural discourse: the case of Yukio Ninagawa." (Critical Essay). *Shakespeare Bulletin*. Winter, 2004, Vol. 22 (4), 2004, pp. 7–24.

Kennedy, Dennis. *Looking at Shakespeare: A Visual History of Twentieth-Century Performance*. 2nd Edition. UK: Cambridge University Press, 2001, pp. 296–300.

Kishi, Tetsuo (1998). "Japanese Shakespeare and English Reviewers." In Takashi Sasayama, J. R. Mulryne, and Margaret Shewring. Eds. *Shakespeare and the Japanese Stage*. Cambridge: Cambridge UP. pp. 110–123.

Lichte, Fischer Erika. *The Show and the Gaze of Theatre: A European Perspective*. Iowa: University of Iowa Press, 1997.

Lan, Yong Li. (2005). "Shakespeare and the Fiction of the Intercultural." In Barbara Hodgdon and W. B. Worthen. Eds. *A Companion to Shakespeare and Performance*. Oxford: Blackwell, pp. 527–549.

Pavis, Patrice. *The Intercultural Performance Reader*. London and Routledge, 1996.

Pronko, Leonard C. (1996). "Approaching Shakespeare through Kabuki." In Minoru Fujita and Leonard Pronko, eds. Shakespeare: East and West. Surrey: Japan Lib. pp. 23–40.

Ryuta, Minami, Carruthers, Ian & Gillies, John. Eds. (2001). "Interview with Ninagawa Yukio." *Performing Shakespeare in Japan*. Cambridge: Cambridge UP, pp. 208–219.

Shakespeare, William. "The Tragedy of Hamlet, Prince of Denmark." *The Riverside Shakespeare*. Boston: Houghton Mifflin Company, 1974, pp. 1135–1197.

Shilling, Jane. "Ninagawa Company's *Hamlet*: Barbican, review: moments of revelation." *The Telegraphy*. Posted on May 22, 2015. http://www.telegraph.co.uk/culture/theatre/theatre-reviews/11619191/Ninagawa-Companys-Hamlet-Barbican-review-moments-of-revelation.html. Retrieved on June 12, 2015.

Yo, Zushi. "Forks in the road come suddenly. I take the dangerous route": Yukio Ninagawa, theatre director. (The NS Interview) (Interview) *New Statesman*. (1996), June 18, 2012, Vol. 141 (5110), p. 38(2).

Websites

Yukio Ninagawa at the Internet Movie Database.
NINAGAWA STUDIO WEBSITE.
Audience reception in Taiwan. Milanhime. http://milanhime.pixnet.net/blog/post/30785914-2015%E8%A7%80%E5%8A%87--%E8%9C%B7%E5%B7%9D%E5%B9%B8%E9%9B%84%E3%80%8A%E5%93%88%E5%A7%86%E9%9B%B7%E7%89%B9%E3%80%8B-hamlet-by-yukio-n. Posted on March 26, 2015. Retrieved on June 16, 2015.

Chapter 5

Case, Sue-Ellen. 1998. *Feminism and Theatre*. New York: Routledge.

Chang, Chen-Chou. 2015. *PAR: Performing Arts Review*. (《表演藝術雜誌》). https://www.artsticket.com.tw/CKSCC2005/Product/Product00/ProductsDetailsPage.aspx?ProductID=oK4bYlG1Gfw2l5nOQcInDQ. Retrieved on June 27, 2016.

Dolan, Jill. 1989. "In Defense of the Discourse: Materialist Feminism, Postmodernism, Poststructuralism and Theory." *The Drama Review* 33: 69.

———. "Ideology in Performance: Looking through the Male Gaze." *The Feminist Spectator as Critic*. Ann Arbor: UMI Research Press, 1988.

Forte, Jeanie. "Focus on the Body: Pain, Praxis, and Pleasure in Feminist Performance." *Critical Theory and Performance*. Ed. Janelle G. Reinelt and Joseph R. Roach. Ann Arbor: The University of Michigan Press, 1992, pp. 248–262.

Goodman, Lizbeth, and Gay, de Jane. *The Routledge Reader in Politics and Performance*. London: Routledge, 2000.

Program. 2015. *To Send Away Under Escort*(押解). Taipei: Greenray Theatre Company.

Fu, Yu-Hui. 2015. Performance Review. https://www.artsticket.com.tw/CKSCC2005/Product/Product00/ProductsDetailsPage.aspx?ProductID=oK4bYlG1Gfw2l5nOQcInDQ. Retrieved on June 27, 2016.

Tuan, Tsai-Hua. 2006. *Selection of Tuan, Tsai-Hua's Novels*. (《段彩華小說選集》). Taipei: The Commercial Press, Ltd.

Yen, Hung-Ya. 2016. *New Millennium Taiwan Theater*. Taipei: Wunan.

Liu, Wan-Chun. 2015. "Greenray Theatre Company's *To Send Away Under Escort* Tour Performance." *Liberty Times*. Posted on Nov. 5. http://www.greenray.org.tw/yajie/news.html. Retrieved on June 27, 2016.

CHAPTER 6

Albrow, Martin. "Modernity at Large: Cultural Dimensions of Globalization by Arjun Appadurai." *American Journal of Sociology*, 103(5): March 1998, pp. 1411–1412.
Appadurai, Arjun. *Modernity at Large: Cultural Dimensions of Globalization*. Minneapolis: University of Minnesota Press, 1996.
Baudrillard, Jean. 2008. "Simulation." Performance Studies. Ed. Richard Schechner, 117–123.
Crocker, Holly A. (Holly Adryan) 2003. "Affective Resistance: Performing Passivity and Playing A-Part in *The Taming of the Shrew*." *Shakespeare Quarterly*, 54(2): 142–159.
Huston, J. Dennis. 1967. "To Make a Puppet." *Shakespeare Studies*, vol. 9: 73, p. 15.
Hutcheon, Linda. *A Theory of Adaptation*. New York and London: Routledge, 2006.
Kislan, Richard. 1995. "The Musical: A Look at American Musical Theater." British Library Cataloging—in- Publication.
Krims, Marvin B. 2002. "Uncovering hate in The Taming of the Shrew" Sexuality & Culture 6.2: 49–64.
Lichte, Fischer Erika. 2003. "Quo Vadis? Theatre Studies at the Crossroads." *Theatre Journal*, 48–66.
Maguire, Laurie E. 1997. "Culture Control in *Taming of the Shrew*." Rose, Marry B. ed. *Renaissance Drama*: New Series XXVI. Northwestern University Press, 1995, 83–105.

Chinese Materials

Creation Volume of A New Hakka Musical: My Daughter's Wedding. Taipei: Council for Hakka Affairs, 2008.
Editing and Commentaries of A New Hakka Musical: My Daughter's Wedding. Taipei: Council for Hakka Affairs, 2008.
Wang, Jun Ting. "Discussion on the Development of Taiwan Musicals Based on the Western Musical's History and Characteristics." (〈從西方音樂劇的歷史與特質看台灣音樂劇的發展〉) *Taiwan University of Arts* 78 (《藝術學報》) (2006): 165–183.
Chu, Chi-Tien. "The Shaming of the Shrew: the Tricks Taught in the Taming-School." (〈奴顏婢膝:御妻學校中傳授的馴悍秘訣〉) *Journal of Humanities College of Liberal Arts National Chung Hsing University* 37 (2006): 365–379.

Chu, Vivian Ching-Mei. "Sondheim/Prince's "Concept Musical": Creative Methods and Process." (〈桑坦/普林斯的"概念音樂劇"創作方法之研究〉) *International Conference On Performance Art*. (2004).
Lu Chien Chung. "The Virtual Courtship Dance: Comment On the Royal Shakespeare Company's *Taming of the Shrew*." (<虛擬求偶舞-評英國皇家莎士比亞劇團《馴悍記》>) *Performance Art* 92 (《表演藝術》) (2000): 67–69.
Li Chiu Min. "The Musical *Aida*: Rock Fashion and Full of Youth"〈歌舞劇《阿伊達》搖滾時尚洋溢青春〉, *Performance Art Review* 191(《表演藝術雜誌》) (2008): 10–11.
Lin, Alan Ying-nan (林璟南). "Style and Interpretation: Feeling of *Hamlet* and *The Taming Of The Shrew*." (〈風格與詮釋-看《哈姆雷特》與《馴悍記》有感〉) *Performance Art* 92(《表演藝術》) (2000): 62–65.
Chu, Chi Hung. "Musical and the Contemporary Stage Revolution of Our Country." (〈音乐剧与我国当代舞台变革〉) *Yellow Bells* 4(《黃鐘》) (2008): 107–114.
Chiu, Yuan. "From 'Musical Comedy' To 'Musical'." (〈從「音樂喜劇」到「音樂劇」〉) *Music Monthly* 120 (《音樂月刊》) (1994): 140–114.
Keng, Yi Wei (耿一偉). "It's Successful to Make the Audience Laugh: Shakespeare's comedy and The Contemporary Production." (〈但能博得觀眾喜,便是功成圓滿時—莎士比亞喜劇與當代製作〉) *Performance Art Review* 191 (《表演藝術雜誌》) (November 2008): 81–85.
Sun, Pao Yin. "Theatre In Broadway."〈百老汇戏剧面面观〉, *Contemporary Theatre* 1 (《當代戲劇》) (2006): 30–31.
Yeh Ken Chuan. "*My Daughter's Wedding*: This Hakka Dish is not tasty." (<《福春嫁女》-一道不入味的客家小炒>) *Academic Journal of Theatre Dept., National Taiwan University of Arts* 7 (《戲劇學刊》) (2008): 241–243.
Yu, Hsiu Li. "Talking About the Broadway Musicals." (〈漫談百老匯音樂劇〉) *Youth Monthly* 359 (《幼獅月刊》) (1980): 56–57.
Lei, Bi-qi (雷碧琦). "Androgynous In Shakespeare's Comedies." (〈既女又男戲扮裝,玩趣背後破藩籬—莎士比亞喜劇中的雌雄同體〉)*Performance Art Review* 191 (《表演藝術雜誌》) (2008): 88–89.
Hsieh, Camilla Chun-pai (謝君白) "The Strategy to Tame the "Taming of the Shrew": Text and Performance Observation." (<馴服《馴悍記》的策略:文本與表演的觀察>) *Chung-Wei Literary Monthly* 28, no. 9 (《中外文學》) (2000): 86–118.

Websites

Project of Culture and Creative Products (文化創意產業計畫) http://web.cca.gov.tw/creative/page/main_03.htm/2008/08/25
Yu, Shan Lu. (于善祿). Comment On the New Hakka Musical *My Daughter's Wedding* (<評新客家歌舞劇《福春嫁女》>) 2007.11.03. http://mypaper.pchome.com.tw/news/yushanlu/3/1297921354/20071103012940/2008/03/25

Others

Program of a New Hakka Musical: *My Daughter's Wedding*. 2008.
R'Way Broadway: The American Musical. Well Go USA. Inc, 2004.

Video-Audio Materials

My Daughter's Wedding. 2DVDs. Taipei: Council for Hakka Affairs. 2008.
My Daughter's Wedding. 2CDs. Taipei: Council for Hakka Affairs. 2008.
R'Way Broadway: The American Musical Explores the 100-Year History and Evolution of American Art Form. 3DVDs. Well Go USA. Inc. 2004.

Interview

Iris Hsin-chun Tuan. Interviewed Director Jiang Wei-Kuo twice. Taipei. Taipei University of the Arts and National Theatre. Oct. 2007.

CHAPTER 7

Barranger, Milly S. 2004. *Understanding Plays*, 3rd ed. U.S.A.: Pearson Education Editions.
Bhabha, Homi. 1987. "Of Mimicry and Man: The Ambivalence of Colonial Discourse." In *October*, edited by Joan, Douglas Crimp, Rosalind Krauss & Annette Michelson, 317–325. Cambridge: MIT Press.
Bharucha, Rustom. 2002. "Interculturalism and Multiculturalism in an Age of Globalization: Discriminations, Discontents, and Dialogue." In *The Color of Theatre*, edited by Roberta Uno and Lucy Mae San Pablo Buns, 27–38. London and New York: Continuum.
Baudrillard, Jean. "Feigning to Have What One Doesn't." Performativity. Ed. Richard Schechner. *Performance Studies: An Introduction*. London and New York: Routledge, 2002.
Foucault, Michel. *Discipline and Punish: The Birth of the Prison*. Trans. Alan Sheridan. New York: Vintage, 1977.
Greenblatt, Stephen. *Renaissance Self-Fashioning: From More to Shakespeare*. Chicago: University of Chicago Press, first 1980, with a New Preface, 2005.
Schechner, Richard. Ed. *Performance Studies: An Introduction*. London and New York: Routledge, 2002.
Schwartz, Murray M. "Shakespeare through Contemporary Psychoanalysis." *Representing Shakespeare: New Psychoanalytic Essays*. Eds. Murray M. Schwartz and Coppélia Kahn. Baltimore: The Johns Hopkins University Press, 1980.
Wang, Ban. "Reimagining Political Community: Diaspora, Nation-State, and the Struggle for Recognition." 48:3 (2005), pp. 249–271.

Chapter 8

Appadurai, Arjun. 1996. *Modernity at Large: Cultural Dimensions of Globalization.* Minneapolis & London: University of Minnesota Press.
Crespy, A. David. 2003. *Off-Off Broadway Explosion.* Foreword by Edward Albee. New York: Back Stage Books.
Kislan, Richard. 1995. *The Musical: A Look at the American Musical Theater.* New York and London: Applause.
Suskin, Steven. 2001. *Broadway Yearbook 1999–2000.* Oxford and New York: Oxford University Press.
Tuan, Iris Hsin-chun. 2011. "My Daughter's Wedding." *Asian Theatre Journal.* Vol. 28. Num. 2: 573–577.
Yu, Mu. 2012. *Broadway Musical.* (《百老匯音樂劇》). Taipei: Da-Di Press.
Program of *Xiangsi Nostalgia*, Hakka Musical. 2016. Sponsored by Hakka Affairs Council. Produced by Taipei National University of the Arts.
Hakka TV advertisement. https://www.youtube.com/watch?v=C4gHcH4exxY. Retrieved on June 8, 2016.
Chunminmou. 2006. "Review of Rent in Taipei Version." (〈劇評:吉屋出租台北版〉) http://blog.udn.com/chunminmau/347431. Retrieved on June 17, 2016.
Pei-Hsin (培心). 2011. "The Importance of *April Rain* in the History of the Musical in Taiwan." (〈《四月望雨》之於台灣歷史在音樂劇表現的重要性〉) http://artmagazine.com.tw/ArtCritic/article825.html. Retrieved on June 17, 2016. Performance film clips
"Karen Mok—The first female artist plays the Broadway Musical *Rent.*" https://www.youtube.com/watch?v=l57sVhzJXWQ. Retrieved on June 8, 2016.
Jolin & Pao's *PK* (2015) between the pop music and the musical. https://www.youtube.com/watch?v=M4jqk2LFWvA; https://www.youtube.com/watch?v=NNFydaipe3k Retrieved on June 8, 2016.
The Hakka musical "*Xiangsi Nostalgia*" (《香絲 相思》) (2016) Hakka TV advertisement. https://www.youtube.com/watch?v=C4gHcH4exxY Retrieved on June 8, 2016.
Xiangsi Nostalgia. 2016. [Program.] Sponsored by Hakka Affairs Council and produced by Taipei National University of the Arts.

Chapter 9

Bay-Cheng, Sarah. "Digital Historiography and Performance." *Theatre Journal.* Vol. 68. Number 4. Dec. 2016, pp. 507–527.
Elley, D. "Disney High School Musical China." `Review.' *Film Business Asia.* 2010, 10 December.

Ho, W. C. "Democracy, citizenship and extra-musical learning in two Chinese Communities: Hong Kong and Taiwan." *Compare: A Journal of Comparative and International Education.* 33(2), 2003, pp. 155–171.

Liang, Chi-Ming. "Director's Interpretation of the Chinese Rock Musical *Mountains and Seas.*" (In Chinese). March, 2016.

Liang, Chi-Ming. Script of the Chinese Rock Musical "*Mountains and Seas.*" (In Chinese). June 19, 2013.

Kenrick, John. *Musical Theatre: A History.* New York and London: Bloomsbury Academic, 2015.

Kun, F., Pratt, K., Provine, R. C., & Thrasher, A. "A discussion on Chinese National Musical Traditions." *Asian Music.* 12(2), 1981, pp. 1–16.

Landow, George and Delany, Paul. "Hypertext, Hypermedia and The History of The Text." *Multimedia: From Wagner to Virtual Reality.* Eds. Randell Packer and Ken Jordan. New York and London: W. W. Norton & Company, 2001, pp. 225–238.

Lustyik, Katalin. "Disney's High School Musical: Music makes the world go 'round.'" *Interactions: Studies in Communication & Culture.* Volume 4 Number 3, 2013, pp. 239–253.

Packer, Randall. "The *Gesamtkunstwerk* and Interactive Multimedia." *The Aesthetics of The Total Artwork.* Eds. Anke Finger and Danielle Follett. Baltimore: The Johns Hopkins University Press, 2011, pp. 155–167.

邱爱金.〈浅析中国原创音乐剧的发展现状〉《音樂天地》2009 (3), pp. 43–45.

———.〈浅析西方音乐剧对中国音乐剧发展的影响〉《音樂天地》2008(11), pp. 59–60.

CHAPTER 10

Carlson, Marvin. *10,000 Nights: Highlights from 50 Years of Theatre-Going.* Ann Arbor: University of Michigan Press, 2017.

Chen, Kuan-Hsing. "Taiwanese New Cinema." *World Cinema: Critical Approaches.* Ed. John Hill and Pamela Church Gibson. Oxford & New York: Oxford University Press, 2000.

Sala, Massimiliano. Ed. *From Stage to Screen: Musical Films in Europe and United Stages (1927–1961).* Italy: Brepols, 2012.

Suh, Sharon A. *Silver Screen Buddha: Buddhism in Asian and Western Film.* USA: Bloomsbury Academic, 2015.

Mulvey, Laura. "Visual Pleasure and Narrative Cinema." +…

Bay-Cheng, Sarah. "The Influence (and Problems) of Feminist Film Theory in Theater Criticism." *Theater and Film: A Comparative Anthology.* New Haven and London: Yale University Press, 2005.

Websites

Toronto International Film Festival. http://www.tiff.net/tiff/the-great-buddha/ Retrieved on Dec. 12, 2017.

Film Review: 'The Great Buddha+' http://variety.com/2017/film/reviews/the-great-buddha-review-1202566032/ Retrieved on Dec. 12, 2017.

USNEWS. https://www.usnews.com/news/entertainment/articles/2017-10-02/the-great-buddha-grabs-10-golden-horse-nominations. Retrieved on Dec. 12, 2017.

2017 Taipei Film Festival. http://eng.taipeiff.taipei/Latest_s.aspx?FwebID=281a5969-697e-47f0-9e68-72031fc796a6&NewsID=240. Retrieved on Dec. 12, 2017.

IMDb. http://www.imdb.com/title/tt7010412/plotsummary?ref_=tt_ov_pl, Retrieved on Dec. 6, 2017.

Wikipedia. https://en.wikipedia.org/wiki/Abjection. Retrieved on Dec. 6, 2017.

CHAPTER 11

Chen, Kuan-Hsing. "Taiwanese New Cinema." *World Cinema: Critical Approaches*. Ed. John Hill and Pamela Church Gibson. Oxford & New York: Oxford University Press, 2000.

Connors, Clare. *Literary Theory: A Beginner's Guide*. England: Oneworld Publications, 2010.

Hoeveler, Diane. "Frankenstein, Feminism, and Literary Theory," in *The Cambridge Companion to Mary Shelley*. Ed. Esther Schor. UK: Cambridge University Press, 2004: 45–62.

Index[1]

A
Adaptation, 4–8, 15, 22, 23, 25, 27, 30, 31, 33, 43, 51, 52, 59, 67, 69–71, 73, 75–80, 86, 88, 90, 92, 104–107, 111, 113–114, 116, 122, 125–137, 163
Asian-Shakespearean performance, 22, 30

B
Brecht, Bertolt, 13, 46, 159
Broadway Musical, 7, 27, 30–32, 34, 65–72, 75, 85, 92, 106–109, 114, 122, 126, 129, 131, 132, 137, 162, 163

C
Chinese Musical, 1, 3, 8, 52, 82, 107, 110, 112, 125–137, 163
Chinglish, 46
Chung, Lihe, 6, 7, 98–100, 102, 103

Contemporary Legend Theatre (CLT), 3, 4, 162
Creolization, 16, 162
Cultural flow, 3, 12, 13, 32, 33, 43, 99, 106
Cultural mobility, 4, 6, 7, 12, 16, 26, 32–34, 66, 92, 97–99, 103, 104, 106, 162, 163
Cyrano de Bergerac, 44

D
Dance, 1, 6–8, 15, 28, 29, 55, 65, 66, 68–71, 73, 75, 79–81, 85, 91, 100–104, 107, 111, 112, 114–116, 118, 119, 122, 126–131, 133–136, 163
Deterritorialized, 32, 34, 99, 106, 162
Diasporic, 3, 33, 106

E
East–West Fusion Theater, 40

[1] Note: Page numbers followed by 'n' refer to notes.

© The Author(s) 2018
I. H. Tuan, *Translocal Performance in Asian Theatre and Film*,
https://doi.org/10.1007/978-981-10-8609-0

175

F
Feminism, 12–16, 54–55, 70, 80, 155, 156, 162
Film, 1–3, 6–9, 12–15, 25, 40, 42, 43, 47, 52, 64, 65, 69, 97–104, 113, 128–130, 132, 140, 141, 143–147, 151–160, 163, 164

G
Godot Theatre, 7, 8, 24, 69, 107, 108, 110, 111, 114, 126, 132
Greenray Theatre Company, 5, 52, 53, 56

H
Hakka, 1, 2, 5–8, 63–92, 97–103, 106, 109, 111, 112, 116–122, 132, 154, 163
Hakka culture, 5–7, 63–64, 66, 70–72, 75, 77, 80–85, 89, 92, 97–104, 120, 163
Hakka image, 70, 97–104, 119, 122, 163
Hakka opera, 1, 6, 63–92, 103, 163
Hamlet, 4, 22, 24, 38–48, 162
Henry IV, 41
Historicalization, 31, 68
Hotspur, 41
Huaju, 24, 25, 57
Hybridity, 3, 14, 14n3, 33, 106

I
Ideoscapes, 33, 99, 106
Intercultural, 1, 3–5, 14, 14n3, 16, 22, 31–34, 38–48, 70–72, 85, 106, 132, 146, 161, 162
Intercultural adaptation, 31
Interculturalism, 14, 16, 162
Intercultural performance, 14n3, 32, 34, 38, 47, 48, 162

Intercultural theatre, 45
Intertextuality, 5, 57
Irresistible, 2, 103, 105–122, 163

K
Kabuki, 4, 34, 39, 40, 44, 48, 162
Kingdom of Desire, 24, 27, 32, 34, 38n2, 162
Kong-Fu, 68
Kunju, 22, 34, 162

L
Literature, 1, 2, 5, 12, 13, 23n1, 24, 32, 51–59, 90, 101, 103, 127, 132, 136, 156, 163
Local, 3–8, 15, 16, 23, 25, 31, 33, 34, 45, 46, 55–56, 67, 69–72, 75–77, 80, 85, 92, 104–107, 109, 111, 112, 114, 116, 119, 120, 122, 130–132, 136, 140, 159, 164
Love's Labour's Lost, 51

M
Macbeth, 22, 24, 38n2, 40, 43, 44
Mahabaharata, The, 45
Mediascapes, 33, 99, 106
Meiji period, 4, 39, 41, 44
Midsummer Night's Dream, A, 3, 4, 22, 23, 25–27, 30–34, 39, 162
Mise-en-scène, 4, 40, 78, 89, 112, 133, 134
Mnouchkine, Ariane, 14n3, 22, 40, 43
Modernity, 3, 12, 65, 72, 85, 102, 106, 162
Montage, 52
Mouse Trap, The, 4, 39, 40, 47
Multi-arts, 7, 8, 105–122, 163
Musical, 1, 2, 5–8, 24, 27, 30, 32, 63–92, 103, 105–122, 125–126, 128–133, 136, 137, 161, 163

INDEX

Musical Theatre, 137
My Daughter's Wedding, 6, 7, 65, 66, 69, 71–76, 78, 80, 84, 85, 91, 92, 112, 113, 116, 119, 121, 122, 163
My Native Land, 98–100

N
Ninagawa, Yukio, 4, 22, 37–48, 162

O
Opera, 1, 3–5, 7, 22–23, 34, 55, 64, 67–69, 83, 85, 86, 88–91, 106, 113, 114, 126, 128, 132, 133, 154
Orientalism, 43, 45

P
Peking opera, 1, 3–5, 22–23, 26, 27, 30, 32–34, 57, 64, 68, 71, 86, 118, 162
Performance Workshop, 24
Performativity, 16, 45, 65, 66, 85
Politics, 2, 5, 9, 48, 52, 55, 56, 70, 147, 151–160, 162, 164
Postcolonial, 2, 12–16, 70, 107, 144, 162

R
Representation, 4, 5, 9, 23, 33, 38–48, 54, 70, 84, 86, 145
Retheatricalization, 47, 70, 88
Richard II, 22, 40
Romeo and Juliet, 24, 43, 115

S
Scapes, 2, 12
Sexuality, 8, 55, 125–137, 145, 163

Shakespeare, William, 3–8, 22–32, 34, 38, 39, 41, 43–48, 43n5, 51, 65–67, 69–76, 79, 85, 91, 92, 107, 113, 115, 116, 121, 162–164
Shamlet, 24, 25, 46
Shingeki, 4, 25, 39, 39n4, 41
Spectacle, 8, 44–48, 81, 86, 118, 119, 122, 125–137, 141–143, 162, 163
Sue-San Being Sent Under Escort, 5, 55, 57

T
Taming of the Shrew, The, 6–8, 24, 65–67, 70, 71, 73–77, 80, 91, 92, 107, 113, 116, 163
Tempest, The, 24, 34, 38n2, 39, 44
Theatricalization, 2, 7, 47, 57, 70, 88, 92, 101, 103
To Send Away Under Escort, 5, 51–59, 163
Translation, 2, 7, 8, 16, 46, 67, 77, 105–122, 132, 163
Translocal, 1–4, 6, 8, 16, 34, 63, 65, 66, 69–71, 80–81, 85, 92, 103–122, 162–164
Translocality, 2, 3, 5, 7, 8, 13–16, 97, 99, 103, 104, 106, 107, 148, 162–164

W
Wenhuaju, 25
Wenmingxi, 25

X
Xinju, 25

Y
Yueju, 22, 34, 162

CPSIA information can be obtained
at www.ICGtesting.com
Printed in the USA
LVHW01*1211130518
577031LV00012B/650/P